Your Horoscope 2021

....

Pisces

20 February – 20 March

igloobooks

Published in 2020
by Igloo Books Ltd
Cottage Farm
Sywell
NN6 0BJ
www.igloobooks.com

0820 001
2 4 6 8 10 9 7 5 3 1
ISBN 978-1-83852-320-6

Written by Belinda Campbell and Denise Evans

Cover design by Simon Parker
Edited by Bobby Newlyn-Jones

Printed and manufactured in China

CONTENTS
· · · · · · · · · · · · · · · · ·

INTRODUCTION
· · · · · · · · · · · · · · · · ·

This 15-month guide has been designed and written to give a concise and accessible insight into both the nature of your star sign and the year ahead. Divided into two main sections, the first section of this guide will give you an overview of your character in order to help you understand how you think, perceive the world and interact with others and – perhaps just as importantly – why. You'll soon see that your zodiac sign is not just affected by a few stars in the sky, but by planets, elements, and a whole host of other factors, too.

The second section of this guide is made up of daily forecasts. Use these to increase your awareness of what might appear on your horizon so that you're better equipped to deal with the days ahead. While this should never be used to dictate your life, it can be useful to see how your energies might be affected or influenced, which in turn can help you prepare for what life might throw your way.

By the end of these 15 months, these two sections should have given you a deeper understanding and awareness of yourself and, in turn, the world around you. There are never any definite certainties, but with an open mind you will find guidance for what might be, and learn to take more control of your own destiny.

THE CHARACTER OF THE TWO FISH

. . . .

Compassionate, creative, and charitable, Pisceans are the visionary dreamers who can breathe magic into the world. Whether it's their love of illusions like Derren Brown or their wonderful world building talents like Dr. Seuss, the enchanting Pisces can help bring joy and expand the minds of others. Neptune and Jupiter co-rule Pisces and provide this sign with a limitless imagination and a thirst for growth. At times, Pisceans can get lost in their fantasies and become detached from reality. A helping hand of support and encouragement from their friends and family might be needed to bring a lost Pisces back to reality. Wherever a Piscean's passion lies, however, their imagination will shine through, from Paul Hollywood's baking, to Michelangelo's Sistine Chapel and even to Albert Einstein's Theory of Relativity.

A Piscean's negative energy means that they can be more focused on their internal growth than on experiencing external stimulus. This means that mental, spiritual and emotional journeys are where this sign most likes to travel. The Two Fish that symbolise this sign can hint at a dual and slippery nature that makes this elusive siren of the sea hard to pin down. As a water sign that is governed by their emotions, they can get carried away on a fast-moving current and should be careful not to drown their loved ones in their, at times, overwhelming excitement. Belonging to the twelfth house in the zodiac calendar where sacrifice and devotion are key, there is surely no sign that is more generous with their time and love than pious Pisces. However, this sign should be careful that their self-sacrificing tendencies don't turn them into a martyr, as Pisceans can have a reputation for becoming or playing the victim at times. As the snow begins to melt and the daffodils bloom, mutable Pisceans are born and bring with them a wise understanding of what has come before. Born at the end of winter and the end of the zodiac calendar, Pisces can be the most adaptable and understanding of all the signs, having learnt something from each of the star signs before them.

THE TWO FISH

Symbolised by the Two Fish, Pisces is one of the signs of the zodiac calendar with a dual symbol. The duality of Pisces could suggest flexibility in their emotions; getting excited for a project one day and bored the next may be all too familiar to many Pisceans. But being the last of the water signs, the Two Fish of Pisces can be capable of exploring the true depth and stretch of their emotions, encompassing both the allure of seductive Scorpio and sensitivity from family orientated Cancer. These slippery Fish can try and wriggle their way out of tight spots, coming up with the most fantastical of fibs. But if a reluctant Piscean constantly swims away from the truth, they may end up going in circles like their symbol of the Two Fish chasing each other's tales. This sign should try to remember that by accepting their slip-ups they can then learn from them and avoid making the same mistakes in the future.

JUPITER AND NEPTUNE

Co-ruled by the largest planet in the sky, Jupiter, and imaginative Neptune, Pisceans can certainly dream big. Jupiter, the ruler of the Gods in Roman mythology, ruled over the sky whilst his brother Neptune ruled the seas. This suggests that Pisceans can be a double force to be reckoned with. At times dreamy, Pisceans may have their heads stuck in their Jupiter clouds and at others they can feel as deeply as Neptune's waters and be as elusive and mythical as a mermaid. Jupiter is the fastest spinning planet in the solar system resulting in it having the shortest days of all the planets, which a tardy Piscean might be quick to blame for their lateness. Pisceans can be incredibly understanding, but when pushed too far their anger can be as tempestuous as the sea of their co-ruler Neptune. Neptune is associated with spiritual intuition and its rule can help guide this compassionate water sign to better understand the world, whilst adventurous Jupiter can help them explore and find their place within it.

ELEMENTS, MODES AND POLARITIES

Each sign is made up of a unique combination of three defining groups: elements, modes and polarities. Each of these defining parts can manifest themselves in good and bad ways and none should be seen as a positive or a negative – including the polarities! Just like a jigsaw puzzle, piecing these groups together can help illuminate why each sign has certain characteristics and help us find a balance.

ELEMENTS

Fire: Dynamic and adventurous, signs with fire in them can be extroverted. Others are naturally drawn to them because of the positive light they give off, as well as their high levels of energy and confidence.

Earth: Signs with the earth element are steady and driven with their ambitions. They make for a solid friend, parent or partner due to their grounded influence and nurturing nature.

Air: The invisible element that influences each of the other elements significantly, air signs will provide much-needed perspective to others with their fair thinking, verbal skills and key ideas.

Water: Warm in the shallows and freezing as ice. This mysterious element is essential to the growth of everything around it, through its emotional depth and empathy.

MODES

Cardinal: Pioneers of the calendar, cardinal signs jump-start each season and are the energetic go-getters.

Fixed: Marking the middle of the calendar, fixed signs firmly denote and value steadiness and reliability.

Mutable: As the seasons end, the mutable signs adapt and give themselves over gladly to the promise of change.

POLARITIES

Positive: Typically extroverted, positive signs take physical action and embrace outside stimulus in their life.

Negative: Usually introverted, negative signs value emotional development and experiencing life from the inside out.

PISCES IN BRIEF

The table below shows the key attributes of Pisceans.
Use it for quick reference and to understand more about this fascinating sign.

SYMBOL	RULING PLANET	MODE	ELEMENT	HOUSE
Two Fish	Jupiter and Neptune	Mutable	Water	Twelfth

COLOUR	BODY PART	POLARITY	GENDER	POLAR SIGN
Sea Green	Feet	Negative	Feminine	Virgo

ROMANTIC RELATIONSHIPS

· · · · · · · · · · · · · · · · ·

Pisceans are the romantics of the zodiac and will no doubt fantasise about being swept off their feet, just like the starry-eyed characters from their favourite romance novels and films. Their intoxicating imagination and endless generosity rarely fail to charm so they are not likely to be short of admirers. As a mutable and self-sacrificing sign, overly generous Pisceans can be at risk of being too agreeable. Pisces should try not to just be the passenger in their relationships and instead take an active role in their love life. Sitting in the driving seat and taking on more responsibilities, whether it's choosing a restaurant for dinner or sorting out the home insurance, could boost an unsure Piscean's self-confidence and give their partner a needed break from always making the decisions.

As a mutable water sign, Pisceans can be adaptable to their partner's emotional needs and highly intuitive lovers. A Piscean's mutable quality means that they are also prone to the desire for change, which can have this sign flipping between their emotions and struggling to bind to just the one lover. Symbolised by not one but two fish makes Pisces a dual sign that is prone to going back and forth, changing their mind and their feelings. Whilst the Two Fish are deciding on a partner who is best suited to them, they may have a few contenders in the running and they can unintentionally hurt their potential spouses if there is any deceit going on. If this sign can stick to the truth, then they should stand a better chance of staying out of hot water with their lovers. Under the philosophical influence of Jupiter and the spiritualism of Neptune, an easy-going Piscean might have a que será, será attitude when it comes to being with someone or not and could be happy to leave it up to the universe to decide for them.

ARIES: COMPATIBILITY 2/5

Dreamy Pisces and action-loving Aries can learn a lot from each other. Watery Pisces can fear delving into the deep end of their desires and prefer to stay in the warmer, shallower waters of their comfort zone, generally choosing to emotionally support their partners' dreams over their own. Aries will want to help Pisces reach their full potential, but Aries should be wary of offending this water sign as Pisces is known to overflow with emotions when pushed. Pisces can offer much needed emotional support to Aries and the two can form a thoughtful connection deeper than most.

TAURUS: COMPATIBILITY 3/5

Taurus and Pisces are capable of having a highly sympathetic and understanding love. The practically minded Taurus should encourage the dreamy Pisces to live out their fantasies and work hard for themselves, not just others. In return, a Piscean will shower their Taurus in waves of love and gratitude for helping them realise their dreams. However, a Piscean would be wise not to saturate the relationship emotionally and spoil a Taurus. With Pisces being a water sign, Taureans can feel the nourishing effects this sign has in their earth element, and the life that these two can grow together is one well worth living.

GEMINI: COMPATIBILITY 3/5

As fluid as water and free flowing as air, Pisces and Gemini can experience an extremely flexible and forgiving relationship when these two fall for each other. Both mutable signs, this couple can be highly compatible and will not fight for leadership but rather rule side by side. Whilst these two may not always perfectly understand each other, their open-minded attitudes will help resolve their disagreements. Whilst Gemini is led by the mind influence of Mercury, contrastingly, the Piscean's influence of water means that they can be ruled by their emotions. A meeting of the head and heart will be key.

CANCER: COMPATIBILITY 4 /5

These two feminine and water signs can be a vision of romance together. A Cancerian can truly identify with the changeable river of emotion that runs within Pisces, alternating speeds, directions and temperatures, because the same river runs within them too. Here are two signs that enjoy nurturing their loved ones and so their love will be built on a mutual support system. Be mindful not to drown in the floods of emotions that both the Crab and Fish are capable of unleashing in their romantic relationships so that love and compassion can flow gently.

LEO: COMPATIBILITY 2/5

When Leo meets Pisces, each can bring out the best and worst in each other. Pisces can be a source of emotional encouragement for Leo, whilst Leo can help the dreamy Pisces take more action in their life. This allows them both to realise their dreams. Born in the twelfth house representing sacrifice, Pisces can be selfless whilst Leo, ruled by the Sun, can be the opposite. When these two sacrificing and self-serving characteristics are felt at their extremes, the relationship can turn toxic. However, mutable Pisces and fixed Leo can live in harmony if they both value each other's best qualities.

VIRGO: COMPATIBILITY 5/5

Opposites on the zodiac calendar, hands-on Virgo and mystical Pisces have a loving match but, like any couple, not without their struggles. The slippery Fish symbol of Pisces can hint at an elusiveness that can be attractive or frustrating to steady earth sign Virgo. Water and earth are elements that can create beautiful things together, however, in this couple the emotional Piscean and rational Virgo could be a tricky balancing act. These two are deep souls that can empathise and support one another probably better than any other signs and can happily and devotedly serve one another for endless days.

LIBRA: COMPATIBILITY 1/5

Whilst the enigmatic Pisces and suave Libra might be charmed by each other, theirs is a love that could struggle to reach fruition. Cardinal Libras are more likely to be the initiator in this relationship with mutable Pisceans, however, both signs can be struck with an inability to make decisions and this can leave them treading water; neither sinking nor swimming. Libras will be attracted to the artistic side of the creative Piscean and Pisceans are likely to flourish with the encouragement from their positive Libra partner. Finding a balance between Libra's extrovert and Piscean's introvert nature could allow their romance to bloom.

SCORPIO: COMPATIBILITY 4/5

Here are two water signs that will go to the ends of the Earth, or rather the depths of the oceans, for one another. Pisceans dream of finding that fantasy love and the enigmatic Scorpio can be just that for them, whilst the empathetic Pisces can be the kindred spirit that secretive Scorpios can finally be vulnerable with. A Piscean's mutable nature which flows with change can be at odds with the steadfast approach of a fixed Scorpio, but their differences mean that they have plenty to learn from each other. Emotional security and sensitivity are where these two thrive.

SAGITTARIUS: COMPATIBILITY 3/5

The roaming Sagittarius and the escapist Pisces could end up blissfully running off into the sunset together if they can learn from each other's differences. Both ruled by Jupiter, these two may indeed have been lucky to find one another. Jupiter gives Sagittarians and Pisceans a zest for life and their shared mutable modes will make their relationship open to continuous growth and change. Pisceans can lack the active side that many fire signs have whilst Sagittarians can lack compassion which could clash with this sensitive water sign. By focusing on common interests, this deep pair could go far.

CAPRICORN: COMPATIBILITY 3/5

An earth and water love is bound to be a complimentary match, and the relationship between a Capricorn and Piscean may be about helping each other grow as individuals and flourish as a couple. Capricorn will bring a practical mind and an active spirit with their cardinal nature whilst the mutable Piscean will provide compassion and teach their Goat to be flexible. Both sides can retreat into themselves in times of great focus or reflection, particularly Pisceans if their Goat partner is being overbearing. However, their matching negative energies could form a deep emotional connection with each other and demonstrate true patience and dedication.

AQUARIUS: COMPATIBILITY 2/5

Two very giving signs such as Pisces and Aquarius could happily give themselves to each other in love. Whilst an air and water sign may struggle to understand one another, an Aquarian's intellect combined with the Piscean's compassion can form a relationship that speaks to both the heart and head if flexibility and patience is practised by the pair. A fixed and mutable combination can be a complimentary match, so long as Aquarians don't try to bend the will of their accommodating Piscean partner. The bond that these two can share when at its best can be sincere and spiritually liberating.

PISCES: COMPATIBILITY 2/5

Two Pisceans might easily capture each other's hearts and imaginations, but their easy-going mutable nature might make their feelings for one another struggle to gain traction and form a solid relationship. However, once these two, or four, Fish decide to commit, their love can be full of thoughtful gift giving and deep emotional understanding. These two water signs can be sponge-like with both positive and negative energies, so could bring out the best and worst in each other, depending on what they offer to the relationship, but at their shared core is a kind and patient soul.

FAMILY AND FRIENDS

....

As a water sign, Pisceans can be incredibly intuitive to the needs of their family and friends, attuned to picking up on even the slightest of changes in their loved one's emotions. A caring Piscean will not think twice about dropping what they are doing to go to a friend's aid, as is their self-sacrificing way. The kind words of a Piscean can help heal many emotional wounds as they will often know just what to say, much to the relief of their family and friends. This eternally compassionate sign is only too glad to give themselves to others that need their support. Kindred spirits for Pisceans are the friends and family that reciprocate their support and encouragement. Fellow water sign Cancer could be a strong ally with their emotional sensitivity and cardinal go-getter attitude helping Pisceans make their dreams into a reality.

Whilst this sign is devoted to their family and friends, sticking to commitments can be a challenge for many slippery Pisceans. This sign should be wary of over-promising and consequently under-delivering in their eagerness to please and inability to say no. It may seem backwards to a Piscean that by saying 'no' they could strengthen the bonds that they cherish, however, their friends and family are far less likely to get angry if they say they cannot make a date straight away rather than flaking at the last minute. Time management is a skill that might not come naturally to this sign, but it is a tool that they should learn how to handle so that they can stay on top of their social calendar. Whilst writing and checking their appointments in a diary or calendar on their phone might not spark the imagination of a Pisces, it will make sure that they don't miss out on spending quality time with their loved ones.

FAMILY AND FRIENDS

Pisceans can be incredibly creative individuals, and this can be reflected in their enchanting homes. Their walls may be adorned with dreamy watercolour paintings or visitors might be greeted with aromas of burning incense to welcome them into a spiritual Piscean's home. A home by the sea or lake, where a Piscean can see their element of water regularly, may be where this sign decides to settle. Wherever a Pisces lives geographically, as a parent this sign can feel truly at home. The imaginative Pisces will want to fill their children's childhood with magic and wonder, making sure that Rudolph takes a bite from his carrot on Christmas Eve or leaving a coin and perhaps a tiny note from the Tooth Fairy. Pisceans, whilst not generally materialistic themselves, can be tempted to spoil their children and will always put their children's needs before their own, but they should be careful of giving or doing too much for them. Whether they are a parent, friend, cousin or sister, a Piscean is ready to bring magic to the lives of others and emotionally support their loved ones.

MONEY AND CAREERS

....

Being a certain star sign will not dictate the type of career that you have, although the characteristics that fall under each sign could help you identify the areas in which you could potentially thrive. Conversely, to succeed in the workplace, it is just as important to understand what you are good at as it is to know what you are less brilliant at so that you can see the areas in which you will need to perhaps work harder in to achieve your career and financial goals.

Whilst Pisceans can have fantastic dreams about what careers they would like to have, they can lack the drive to make their fantasies a reality. A Piscean can get so blissfully lost in thinking about their dream job that they fail to take the necessary steps to reach their goals especially if they are in the habit of underestimating themselves, but building their self-confidence usually helps them to take action. A compatible career path for Pisceans would be something that sparks their imagination and gets their creative juices flowing. Whether it's the music of Rihanna or the paintings of Renoir, a creative Piscean could look to aspirational figures that inspire them to turn their passion into a paid career. Another professional path that Pisces may prefer to follow is one where they can dedicate their time and energy towards improving the lives of others. Born in the twelfth house that signifies service and sacrifice, Pisces can be some of the kindest and most generous of souls, so a caring career as nurse, aid worker, or foster parent could be best suited to the giving Pisces.

When it comes to a Piscean's finances, money can pass through their fingers as quickly as their element water. This sign will not hesitate to buy something that catches their fancy which can start to be an issue when they unwittingly spend beyond their means. The creative Piscean may have unsteady income and not have much of a grip on their finances and the all too real world of budgets. If the mere thought of spreadsheets is bringing a Piscean out in hives, they would do well to pay for someone else to help with their expenses, particularly if they are self-employed. Earth signs like Taurus, Virgo, and Capricorn will usually have a flair for material things and their practical approach could help a disorganised Pisces handle their money more frugally, helping them establish boundaries to manage their incomings and outgoings. Whilst trusting Pisceans may be tempted to believe in a magical fix to their financial worries, they should avoid any get-rich-quick type schemes as if it sounds too good to be true, it probably is.

Whilst you can't always choose who you work with, it can be advantageous to learn about colleagues' key characteristics through their star signs to try and work out the best ways of working with them. As a water sign, Pisceans can be swept up in negative and positive energies from their colleagues so it's important for this sign to surround themselves with the latter and guard themselves against the former. Pisceans truly thrive on positive encouragement, so their neighbouring sign of Aquarius could be the optimistic and creative influence that helps a Piscean to reach their career dreams.

HEALTH AND WELLBEING

. . . .

Pisceans can be the ultimate escapism artists, living in their own fantasy and choosing to be blind to any painful issues in their real life. But even with lucky Jupiter co-ruling this sign, their problems won't often magically fix themselves. If a Piscean feels themselves drifting into escapism, binging on films or playing video games at all hours, then they will need to make a strong conscious effort to come back to reality. Whilst this sign may blame others for their upset state, they could also be a victim of their own making. Pisceans feel deeply, and as a negative sign can internalise their distress. As a sensitive water sign, learning to let go of any emotional pain from the past and focusing on the positives of the present will do wonders for their wellbeing. Practising mindfulness through meditation can be a useful tool for a spiritual Piscean to ease their anxieties and bring them back to a present state of calm.

Self-love is important for every sign, but Pisceans can easily forget to nurture themselves whilst they are busy looking after everyone else. Taking time to indulge their creative side can be essential to a Piscean's happiness, but is something they sometimes sacrifice for the sake of others. If a Piscean has an artistic talent, be it with words, art, music, food, or anything else, they should indulge in their creativity and enjoy the healing magic that they can create. Taking time for themselves may have the consequence of having less time for others, which can feel selfish to this giving sign, but taking even an hour to enjoy a bath, read a book, or hone their chosen art is vital for this sign's health and wellbeing. Once a depleted Piscean has been able to recharge their batteries, they will

· · · · · · · · · · · · · · · · · ·

find that they are able to give much more of themselves to the world as a direct result.

Physical activity is a key way for everyone to stay fit, no matter their star sign, but Pisceans can be more interested in stretching their imagination than they are their bodies. If Pisces wants to get into a good exercise routine, finding a sport or physical activity that they enjoy and can be creative in will be important. As a water sign, Pisces could quite literally be in their element whilst swimming, surfing, or ice skating. If water or an ice rink aren't readily accessible to this sign, their associated body part, feet, could have them dancing their way to fitness in a Zumba class or at their favourite music club. Pisceans will no doubt appreciate the creativity of music and dance and getting healthier will just be a happy bonus for them. Whilst it might be tempting for a Pisces to stick on their best heels before hitting the dance floor, wearing comfier footwear could save them some plasters and keep their associated body part happy and healthy.

Pisces

. . . .

DAILY FORECASTS
for 2020

OCTOBER

Thursday 1st

October begins with a Full Moon in your money sector. This will highlight a few things from the last six months. The most important thing here is that your sense of self-worth is showing itself now. You have worked hard on boundary issues and not being walked over. Make sure it stays that way.

Friday 2nd

Venus, the planet of love and harmony, enters your relationship sector. This is great news for you. Venus will see that your love relationships are balanced and harmonised while she is here. Pay attention to all the subtle love nuances now. Happy days!

Saturday 3rd

A delicious connection from the Moon to Venus means that romance is most definitely in the air today. Good food, wine and company are on the menu for a sensual evening. If you are single then indulge yourself with all your favourites.

Sunday 4th

You have a pause from your romantic place today. The Moon sits opposite Mercury, who wants to delve deep into another person's secrets. You may be holding back a bit now and this will cause a wobble in your vulnerable love-life. Choose how far to go, remember boundaries.

Monday 5th

Good news, Pluto is now direct. If you have learned the lesson of not giving your power away to everyone, then this shift will be welcome in your love life. Someone is inviting you to be more intimate, can you do this without falling back on old habits?

Tuesday 6th

The telephones buzz today as your family are ever active and chatty. Maybe someone has news and all the family are sharing this at the same time. You enjoy the random, light-hearted conversations with siblings. You will even enjoy the teasing and mock fighting. You have a very communicative family.

Wednesday 7th

Mercury sits opposite Uranus today and this influence means that you have to watch what you say. This can be Mercury motormouth speaking out of turn. It can also mean that he has probed too far and is being given a warning to back off. Please respect this.

Thursday 8th

The Moon slips into a more nurturing sign which, for you, is covered by your creative sector. Today, try to do things which are soul food for you. Creative expression in the form of art or poetry would be good. Better still, dedicate this to a muse and thrill your lover.

Friday 9th

You may find that control issues surface today but you know how to deal with this now, don't you? Saying 'no' from a place of compassion leads to the greatest respect for both parties. The Moon and Venus help you to do this. Well done, what a transformation.

Saturday 10th

Your lover may surprise you today with another evening out. Venus connects to Uranus in a helpful way which means that surprises, not shocks, will occur. You may be making many trips and messages in the day but the evening will be sensual and relaxing. Nurture your taste-buds now.

Sunday 11th

Be careful today. You or someone close to you can be rather unstable emotionally. Be kind and thoughtful, as this is just a passing moon phase and will not last. It has no basis in reality and is therefore not a serious issue. Do not dig for answers.

Monday 12th

Mercury is soon to go on another retrograde mission so today, remember to back up your devices and double-check travel plans. Now is not the time to sign new contracts or make commitments. Bide your time as this retrograde will cover sectors dealing with deep issues and shared finances.

Tuesday 13th

The Moon enters your relationship sector now. Try not to make too many plans with a loved one as they are likely to be disrupted. Keep it low-key, close to home and on a level that will not cause any unrest. Take it slowly and keep the fire on a low burn.

Wednesday 14th

Mercury retrograde begins. The Moon and Venus sit together to watch the show from your relationship sector. A simple romantic comedy is just the thing for a mid-week rendezvous. Nothing fancy or expensive. Simply a homely, uncomplicated evening with food and a movie. Make everyone's favourite comfort foods.

Thursday 15th

What have you learned concerning power struggles, this year? This may be the first test from Pluto, and in a Mercury retrograde too! Pluto needs to see something demolished and rebuilt. This is a time of endings and beginnings. Consider what has outlived its usefulness in your life now.

Friday 16th

Today's New Moon gives you a hint at what needs to be transformed. What is out of balance now? What deep issues do you choose to ignore because you are too scared to deal with them? Balance needs to be restored by your own hands, otherwise Pluto will do it for you.

Saturday 17th

The Moon makes connections to Mercury and Uranus, and this influence will make you say what is on your mind. Mercury is retrograde and in the deep, intense sign of Scorpio. You may push or be pushed too far today. If it is too uncomfortable, don't go there.

Sunday 18th

You will be satisfied with your progress on your mission. Today you can sit back and assess how far you have come. You have changed many things for the better and lightened your load. What an achievement. You can still be the empathic, caring friend but now you know your limits better.

Monday 19th

Venus and Mars are fighting for a bit of Jupiter's good fortune. For you, this means that men and women may be in a friendly challenge today. Women, with Venus' aid, are much more likely to win this one. This battle involves your money sector and your 'other' sector. Which side are you on?

Tuesday 20th

More tense energy today as Mercury retrograde sits opposite Uranus in your money and value sector. There may be rows about what you own and what is shared with another. This is another of the retrograde influences. Keep calm and resist the need to prove yourself right.

Wednesday 21st

Venus is sweet-talking Pluto. She is persuading him that something in your relationship sector needs to change. She wants it done her way and is asking Pluto to help. Watch out for sneaky control issues in your relationship. If it is not that serious, let it happen. You might like it.

Thursday 22nd

The Sun now begins its month-long stay in your travel sector. Here, you will discover a fascination for other cultures, higher education and possibly taboo subjects like sex, death and rebirth. The occult attracts you now. Expand your mind; it will be good for you.

Friday 23rd

You are emotionally driven to be with friendship groups which stand for a good cause today. You get out your soapbox and make a speech loaded with emotion. Your words will fall on deaf ears. Do you really want to raise a revolution? Step down and concentrate on your lover now instead.

Saturday 24th

Venus now turns her attention to Saturn. Someone around you, most likely your lover, will push a little further through your comfort zone. This is OK, because you are learning to accept your limits and will know it when they are triggered. This is a good test of your convictions.

Sunday 25th

Mercury has nothing to say today as he is in the heart of the Sun and listening. The Moon enters your sign and you may feel moodier than usual. This is time for you to drift off into your own world and listen, like Mercury's doing. Connect to your spirit now.

Monday 26th

The Moon in your sign is making helpful connections to the Sun, Mercury and Uranus. You will hear something to your advantage. This could come from deep inside you, or from another person. You may even hear the voice of 'God' now. Keep this information to yourself until the retrograde is over.

Tuesday 27th

The Moon now sits on top of Neptune and further deepens the surreal, spiritual atmosphere going on within you. Do not be fooled by false prophets. You may drift too far today, so do something grounding and stay connected to this planet. Physical exercise or yoga will help.

Wednesday 28th

Today, you have Venus and Mercury both entering your sex, death and rebirth sector from either end. Mercury is of course still retrograde. They appear to call out to each other. Venus wants to know the secrets that Mercury has unearthed. It is crucial that you are discreet today.

Thursday 29th

The Moon pays a visit to sulky Mars in your money sector.
You may have a setback with finances that cause you to regret
some spending from earlier in the year. There is nothing you
can do about it. Get through the day by doing something Mars
likes. Exercise helps.

Friday 30th

You are contemplating your future based on your past.
Conversations with siblings can bring up a lot of memories.
You probably wonder if your current situation is a result
of your past efforts and wind up focusing on the mistakes.
Turn that around and celebrate your successes. Do not dumb
yourself down.

Saturday 31st

A Full Moon in your communications sector brings things
to a conclusion. The Sun opposes Uranus and you get an
'aha' moment. The Moon sits on top of Uranus and you feel it
profoundly. A moment of regret comes over you as you feel a
chapter has exposed itself and is now closing.

NOVEMBER

. . . .

Sunday 1st

There may still be some spooky surprises for you. The Halloween Full Moon has left the Sun shining right in the face of Uranus. You may get a 'Eureka!' moment where something now becomes blindingly obvious. There will be happy communication today, too. You should hear some good news.

Monday 2nd

Your family sector gets triggered today. The Moon connects to Saturn, and it's likely that you will hear some good advice from an elder in the family. Saturn reminds you of your boundaries and is pleased that you are putting them in place. Teachers may also feature.

Tuesday 3rd

A lovely connection between the Moon, Mars and Venus means that interactions between men and women should go well today. Family can be fun and full of laughter, and the mood is likely to be much lighter than it has been. Several generations may gather together. Enjoy each other's company.

Wednesday 4th

Mercury, at last, goes direct again. He will journey back over parts of your sex, death and rebirth sector, then continue his mission in your travel and higher education sector. Maybe you have taken this time to review these areas. Both of these areas are deep and uncomfortable for you.

Thursday 5th

Your love life and artistic pursuits are in the spotlight now.
These could be the same thing. You may be in love with art,
music or literature. There will be a little difficulty getting
things to the standard you desire today. Don't lose heart; put it
aside for another time.

Friday 6th

Today you may feel tired and have no energy. Your creative
urges are just not going the way you want and it is making
you weary. This is better than making you feel frustrated and
angry, which it could well do. Use this time to rest up and look
again with fresh eyes.

Saturday 7th

Health should be your main topic today. If you have been
cooped up indoors too much lately, take a brisk walk outdoors.
Fresh air will fill your lungs and make you feel good. You may
lead an expedition to a new place. Be child-like today, surprise
yourself.

Sunday 8th

Today's energy is of a fixed nature which will feel
uncomfortable to you, who likes to go with the flow. It will
feel rigid and restrictive. Someone may have made plans that
cannot be changed. There is a danger of you having a tantrum
now. Do what you are told today.

Monday 9th

The Moon enters your opposite sign and your important relationships become your focus. This may not be a good thing, because the celestial lovers are sitting opposite each other and remember, Mars is in retrograde. Women may be persuasive or bossy, but either way they tend to have the upper hand today.

Tuesday 10th

Mercury hits the very last degree of your sex, death and rebirth sector. This area also deals with shared finances. Anything you committed to over the last few weeks is now up for a final review. This is a take-it-or-leave-it time. It is probably best to leave it, but assess this carefully.

Wednesday 11th

You have taken Mercury's advice and are now assessing money that you have tied up with another person. You will be aiming to balance out what is yours and what belongs to someone else. You may find that you are implementing the lessons from the planets in your social sector.

Thursday 12th

The Moon sits with Venus today, and together they help you to reconcile all that may have gone awry during the Mercury retrograde. You are sensitive and loving. Deep feelings come up but they do not bother you. Awareness is the first step to dealing with them.

Friday 13th

Jupiter and Pluto meet in your social sector. This means that big changes can be made without trauma. These changes are likely to be connected to friendships. You handle this exceptionally well. Something old and outworn has become a new thing of beauty. This is a treasure for you.

Saturday 14th

Mars gets his boots back on and turns direct. At last, you see forward motion and become more assertive in the area of money, self-worth and beauty. He is in his own sign and will do his very best for you while he is here. Energy levels should pick up and new projects be started. All systems are go now.

Sunday 15th

Today's New Moon is an excellent time to use that Mars energy to make new plans, intentions and goals. The Moon is in the other sign Mars rules, Scorpio. Anything begun now has a high chance of success. Intensity and power are yours to use if you so choose, now.

Monday 16th

Venus is squaring off to the planets in your social sector, but this time she is not going to get her way. You may find that someone comes creeping back to attempt to renew a friendship with you. You must be strong and stick to your convictions.

Tuesday 17th

You are at a standstill today and looking back at the past, maybe even the recent past. There is a chance of getting into an argument today. Mercury is opposite Uranus which means that everyone needs to watch what they say and think before they speak.

Wednesday 18th

The Moon in your social sector makes an uneasy connection to Mars. Perhaps he is marching onwards and leaving something behind. This will make you feel like you have left good friends behind. March on; you're doing the right thing.

Thursday 19th

The Sun in your travel sector is talking to Saturn. Think about boundaries when Saturn is involved. This time, stretching your boundaries and exploring other lands is the theme. Saturn encourages you to grow within reasonable limits, if it means that you are educated. Where will you go?

Friday 20th

Now is a good time to dream. You have been given a passport by Saturn and you can now explore your fantasies. You are surprised by your urge to go beyond your comfort zones. People may try to dissuade you. This is the time for you to grow in another direction.

Saturday 21st

The Sun now warms up your career sector. This could herald a time where career and travel are combined. You may be asked to go on a business trip. Venus gets sexy in your travel sector today, too. Does the exotic and erotic attract you? Is this your new mission?

Sunday 22nd

The Moon enters your sign and your heart beats a little faster with new ideas. There is something in the air which excites you now. This could be new journeys, courses or a change of career. Whatever it is, it's putting a much-needed spring in your step.

Monday 23rd

The Moon makes lovely connections today which lighten your spirit. She sits with Neptune, who likes to dissolve boundaries. At this time, he is taking down your personal reservations about stepping out further in life. The Moon is also talking to your social sector, do you have friends abroad?

Tuesday 24th

Mercury rather likes this new-found courage of yours and gets all the information from Neptune. He begins to scan the depths of your travel sector and believes that the more unusual cultures will suit you best. The Moon in your money sector looks at the financial side for you.

Wednesday 25th

You may start a savings plan for your new ideas concerning travel or development. Put some money aside and build on it until the time is right. Listen to your dreams now, as they will give you a hint as to where you would benefit the most. Dream symbols are the clues.

Thursday 26th

You are raring to go. The new plans you have been forming in your mind are exciting you. You may feel like a runner at the start of a race, filled with anticipation and adrenaline. Hold back, you are just at the planning stages of this bold new adventure.

Friday 27th

The tension continues as the Moon sits with Uranus, and they both sit opposite Venus. She is bewitching you with tales from exotic lands. You may be frustrated that you cannot do anything about this right now. Uranus gets you jumpy today. Calm down.

Saturday 28th

You have further confirmation that this new, exciting adventure is right for you. Neptune, your co-ruler wants his little fish to swim far and wide. The ocean is far too big to stay only in one place. You have permission to explore the warmer or colder seas.

Sunday 29th

The planets in your social sector now give you their blessings, too. This year's lessons regarding boundaries should have taught you that personal ones must be protected. Now it is teaching you that your world and its physical boundaries are there to be explored. The excitement is building.

Monday 30th

Today, there is a Full Moon in your family sector. Something will come to a head and be completed now. You inform your family of any new plans and receive their encouragement. One warning though, not everyone will be happy for you. A lunar eclipse throws a shadow over you.

DECEMBER

· · · · · · · · · · · · · · · · ·

Tuesday 1st

You get extra help with planning any career moves now, especially if they concern travel. Mercury enters your career sector and will assist you in researching these areas. This will be a fantastic opportunity to put your ideas out there to the boss. Put the feelers out now.

Wednesday 2nd

Nurture yourself with some home comforts. You may also want to spend time on your artistic projects, as these also give you food for your soul. Today is also favourable for snuggling down with a loved one and enjoying each other's company in the safety of your home.

Thursday 3rd

Today, you'll probably find that emotions and actions are not in sync. You'll try to find the enthusiasm to get on with things, but are unlikely to have the energy or inclination. As long as the more important tasks are done, leave the smaller ones for another time.

Friday 4th

Your energy levels have picked up and you will be going about your duty with a cheery smile. Nothing can keep you down for long. The Moon and Mercury are exchanging messages, and both are on task to make your travel and career plans a real possibility.

Saturday 5th

The Moon in your health and duties sector gives Mars the energetic kick he needs. Money talks are possible. Could this be a promotion? Be careful when communicating, as someone may want to rock your boat. There is stubbornness in the air; are you the immovable one? Might others think that you're being unreasonable?

Sunday 6th

Venus is gracing your travel sector with her beauty and harmony. She also rules money. Today she talks to the planet of dreams, Neptune. Together they help you to consider the money options for your next mission. You also think about the pros and cons of such an adventure.

Monday 7th

Today you may need to discuss things with a lover or important person in your life. You will be going over the finer details of your plans. This is a step-up for you, as this is something you don't like doing. This person may surprise you with their experience.

Tuesday 8th

A connection from the Moon to the planets in your social sector encourages you to be with like-minded people. Saturn sits at the final critical degree of this sector for the next ten days. It is crucial that you use this time to review the lessons you have learned on boundaries.

Wednesday 9th

Don't get fooled today. You may become so fixated on something that you fail to see the shortcomings. Bad advice or discouragement may come your way. Step to one side and view this with eyes wide open. Something that is too good to be true usually isn't true.

Thursday 10th

Sexy Venus in your travel sector flirts with Pluto, the planet of change. If you have friends abroad or with great influence, you may connect with these now. There could be an open invitation to visit. Do your homework first, weigh it all up and, if it looks good, go for it.

Friday 11th

The Moon now also enters your travel sector. Be mindful that you can become overly attached to a plan that stirs your emotions. Your interest in the exotic and erotic grows, and you may surprise yourself by finding a new passion in the deeper mysteries of life.

Saturday 12th

The Moon and Venus share the same spot in the sky, and this too is in your travel sector. You may have never before considered foreign culture as something that would attract you but here it is, filling your heart with longing. Mars gives you the energy to focus on the finances you need.

Sunday 13th

This new mission to explore is gifted to you by the planetary positions in your chart. The Moon is in a sign which deals with higher education and foreign travel, but is also in your career sector. Remember Saturn sitting at that last degree? It's time to approach the boss.

Monday 14th

Here's the golden opportunity that you've been waiting for. A New Moon in the sign of travel and the area of career urges you to set this plan in motion. Venus and Jupiter, who are known for their blessing, are connecting and sending you lots of luck.

Tuesday 15th

Beautiful Venus steps into your career sector. What more can you ask for? There will be peace and harmony in the workplace. As she also rules money, this heralds a good time for you to make a solid action plan. Your words and energy are in sync today.

Wednesday 16th

For the next two and a half years, Saturn will be travelling through your sector of dreams and isolation. There will be tough lessons to learn now. You will learn how to be alone, but not lonely. Your inner rebel may surface and there will be good causes that interest you.

· · · · · · · · · · · · · · · · · ·

Thursday 17th

The Moon makes great connections with Jupiter and Saturn today. You will feel gratitude for their influence on you this year. Think of these as the best teachers and guides you can have. Take the time today to acknowledge the gifts they have given you to help you grow.

Friday 18th

Mercury is quiet today as he sits in the heart of the Sun. Now is your chance to listen. Take in all the information you need for future career plans. Research, collate and sort through any data you have gathered which may be of use to you.

Saturday 19th

The Moon enters your sign and you will feel reflective. Jolly Jupiter is at the last degree of your social sector. Today there will be fun with special friends but with Jupiter here, he is just giving you a warning that he expands what he touches. Don't overdo the food and drink!

Sunday 20th

Jupiter says goodbye to your social sector and bounces into your dreams. He will stay here for a year and you will enjoy his many blessings. He greets Saturn as he does so. Fathers and sons may feature, and you will see reconciliation or renewed commitment to elders or authority figures.

Monday 21st

The Winter Solstice occurs today. The longest, darkest night is the best time to reflect on the past year. You will feel sociable and need to get out with friends. Self-sacrifice is your default and you may return to it, but only for a moment.

Tuesday 22nd

The Solstice brought the Sun to your social sector. This is great timing as you will get a good idea of how your friendship circles have now changed for the better. You will become a leader of sorts and great respect comes your way. Well done, be proud of yourself now.

Wednesday 23rd

You may feel a little edgy today. The Moon sits with Mars and you may be spending too much. They both connect to Pluto, who tells you to take control of this spending. It is Christmas and this is quite normal, but your planetary allies cannot help but warn you.

Thursday 24th

Now the eating, drinking and parties are starting. The Moon is in your communications sector and is typically adding to the mood of the season. In this sector, you make many short trips and messages. The Moon here likes the good things in life and you deserve them.

Friday 25th

Happy Christmas. There are so many surprises coming your way. Fathers, sons, friends and lovers will gather today and make your day special. The Moon sits with Uranus, indicating surprise. Be careful, as this may also be tension and irritability. This is all typical of the season.

Saturday 26th

Today you may be recovering from the night before. The Moon connects to Neptune, your co-ruler. Neptune can influence time spent alone in another world. There is also a chance that you are asked to be your old self and self-sacrifice. The Moon also connects to Pluto, who gives you the power to say no.

Sunday 27th

Family time is still on the agenda. Perhaps you have a large family and the season dictates a lot of visits to relatives. Siblings can provide fun and laughter, today. Go with the flow and let your inner child come out to play.

Monday 28th

You will be thinking about, and sharing, your visions and dreams with family now. You may have some resistance from people who think it is a bad move. Listen to what they are saying and respect their opinion, as you are having some guilt about this. Let this mood pass.

Tuesday 29th

Just before the year ends, there is a Full Moon in your creative sector. Mother figures are in the spotlight now. An artistic project, with which you nurture yourself, may have come to completion now and you can celebrate it. Love affairs are also illuminated under this Moon.

Wednesday 30th

How do you nurture and how do you provide? There may be questions today regarding how your new vision of travelling will benefit you financially. You may be thinking if it is even viable. You get a moment of conflicting emotions. Hold onto them, but know that these will pass soon.

Thursday 31st

The end of the year arrives and you take a good look back at 2020. You will feel emotional about the necessary losses of the year. You may not have the energy to party the year away. Be good to yourself and recall how much you have grown. Enjoy 2021.

Pisces

· · · · · · · · · · · · · ·

DAILY FORECASTS
for 2021

JANUARY

. . . .

Friday 1st

Happy New Year and welcome to 2021. Last night's Full Moon may have seen you being your best creative self. Perhaps you have found your muse or new inspiration to write your next chapter. You are now ready to fully express yourself in service to others.

Saturday 2nd

Mundane duties can be joyful today, as your spirits are high and you are happy to get things done. Mars in your money and values sector is asking that you check your bank balance and ensure that you haven't overdone it during the festive season. If you're lucky, there may be cash to spare.

Sunday 3rd

The Moon moves into your relationship sector. You may find that you're analysing situations or people more than usual. A helpful connection to Uranus makes conversations open, free and, at times, controversial. It's possible that you solve a problem with a loved one now. Check all the details.

Monday 4th

The Moon opposes Neptune, your co-ruler in your sign today. You may be dreamy and unrealistic. This is nice if you are reminiscing or being nostalgic, but difficult if you need a clear head in order to make decisions. You may be emotional and immovable today if you can't see the way ahead.

Tuesday 5th

Mercury meets Pluto today in your social sector. This meeting usually implies that you have a new mission on the way. Your self-improvement may involve looking at your wider interest groups and making changes. Don't be led astray by fast-talking pleasure-seekers; manipulation may surface today too.

Wednesday 6th

Mars spends his final day in your finance and value sector. You may need to find your more assertive side and take the lead here. Laying the law down is hard for you, but it may be the only answer today. Be fair, be kind, but be strong.

Thursday 7th

Your communication sector is now visited by Mars. It's likely that his stay here will make you more determined and driven. You may find the pace slow and frustrating, but the results will be more pleasing. You can be too changeable and malleable but with Mars' help; you can be a force to be reckoned with.

Friday 8th

Grounding energy may feel restrictive today. Feel into it, as it will be more than helpful in getting your chores done. You may have difficulty arranging an event with friends, but stick with it and you will succeed. An intense Moon in your travel sector can make you reach out further than before.

Saturday 9th

Mercury now enters your hidden sector. After his meeting with Pluto, you may feel an uncomfortable shift as subconscious material or old wounds can be triggered. You may be edgy today and not know where this is coming from. Try not to say anything you may regret later. Retreat if you need to.

Sunday 10th

Mercury meets the hard taskmaster, Saturn. This may feel like a blockage or even a telling off. Your instincts might be to react as you did as a child. Take note of this, as these outdated responses need to change now. The big retrogrades of this year will see to that.

Monday 11th

Now Mercury meets Jupiter. This will feel like conflicting energy to yesterday and may leave you feeling confused. Jupiter only wants the best for you, but will also have a lesson for you. Your desire to speak may bubble up into an outpouring you come to regret later. You might already feel change happening.

Tuesday 12th

The Moon visits your social sector. You may be more inclined to seek refuge within your friendships now. You have long-standing tight bonds with friends who can influence your mood. Choose wisely now, as you are likely to spill your heart out to anyone who will listen.

Wednesday 13th

A New Moon occurs in your social sector. This is a great time to make new goals and intentions regarding friendships and shared goals. However, other planetary energy is difficult, and you may feel like whichever way you turn, you experience negativity. Remember to be kind to yourself and take a break from outside activities if you need to.

Thursday 14th

The Sun meets Pluto today. You may see manipulation tactics being exposed or ego battles around you and your social circle. It's likely that you feel this quite sharply and you may feel let down by others. Your deep soul issues may take a hit and you might find yourself nursing your wounds.

Friday 15th

You may have time to wallow in self-pity today, but you can still use this time more wisely. Try staring at your demons and sending love to your inner child. You have the knack of finding unusual ways to resolve problems of this kind. Play with ideas now.

Saturday 16th

The Moon enters your sign and lets you choose which way to play. You can be romantic, changeable and elusive if you wish. Others may find you a little too surreal and prefer to see the person with big ideas and inspiration. Take a concept and work on it today.

Sunday 17th

The Moon meets Neptune and you may be in danger of drifting off to a fantasy island in your mind. If you are clever, you may use this energy to connect to your inner compass and follow guidance on your path. Patience and perspective are needed now.

Monday 18th

This morning, you're more active and have plans to see to. You may be busy beautifying your home or spending on improvements. Jupiter, your ruler, squares off with Uranus and makes you uncomfortable again. Deep stuff from your psyche is stirring. Go with the flow and let it happen.

Tuesday 19th

The Sun moves into your hidden sector. This may cause you further discomfort as it will illuminate the very problems you need to work on this year. The active Moon hits a snag with Venus in your social groups, but allows you the power of Mercury to bring all back into harmony again.

Wednesday 20th

Mars and Uranus meet today. This is a powerhouse of very unstable energy in your finances and values sector. You may find yourself rushing to finish a group project; it's also possible that you throw it all up in the air and give up.

Thursday 21st

The Moon joins Mars and Uranus now. You may find that this is an emotional and disruptive day. Conserving your personal energy is important. Don't do more than you must and allow others to take care of you if or when burn-out occurs. Treat yourself to food and company that you enjoy this evening.

Friday 22nd

Try to remain silent and not engage in any outside-the-box conversations today. Venus and Pluto meet the Moon and urge you to look at self-care tactics. You cannot serve everyone else if your own cup is half empty. Your social activities may be nice but draining.

Saturday 23rd

Venus and Neptune make a nice connection to help you realise a few dreams which will be good for you in the short term. Venus represents your desires, so look at what it is you want right now and go get it. Be warned that you may see anger issues around you.

Sunday 24th

The Sun meets Saturn in your hidden sector. Inflated egos may be taken down a peg or two. Saturn will give heavy feelings and a glum outlook, which will be difficult to ignore when the Sun illuminates them. Try to use the Sun energy to lighten heavy feelings instead.

Monday 25th

Family life may be full of chatter and laughter right now, but will soon dip into co-dependency and nurturing. Mars and Jupiter are still struggling and may mean that your self-talk is getting too negative. Let yourself be guided by feminine wisdom and maternal care this evening.

Tuesday 26th

The Moon is in your creative sector and there may be a project that you have been nurturing which is now mature enough to be born. This may also be a love interest. Keep it safe a little while longer. Expect a shock or surprise to be revealed today.

Wednesday 27th

As much as you enjoy being cared for or doing the caring, today it's likely to get too much for you. The Moon opposes Pluto and Venus and you desire to break free. Speaking up for yourself is important now. Let others know if they've overstepped the mark and made you uncomfortable.

Thursday 28th

A lovely Full Moon occurs in your health and duties sector. This will highlight something that has come to fruition in the last six months. It may be that you aren't taking care of yourself or that you're doing more than you can cope with.

Friday 29th

You may not be in the best of moods right now. Understand that this is fleeting energy and will pass soon. The Sun and Jupiter meet today in your hidden sector. This is highly beneficial and will lift your spirits. You may see the hidden gold in your psyche today.

Saturday 30th

Mercury turns retrograde tomorrow, so use today to make all the necessary checks. Double-check travel plans, back up all your devices and refrain from making any commitments. This is a great day to check details and uncover all the facts. Time spent with a lover fulfils you.

Sunday 31st

Mercury retrograde begins in your social sector. Disagreements with friends are likely, as is trouble in the workplace. Keep your eye on the ball for the next three weeks. You may feel that your dreams are impossible now, but they aren't. Your perception is off today; look again tomorrow.

FEBRUARY
. . . .

Monday 1st

Venus enters your hidden sector. You may now find that the uncomfortable shifts in your psyche are tempered with self-love and this will go a long way. You may also find a passion for a good cause or event and wish to be part of a collective who are doing some good in the world.

Tuesday 2nd

Balancing energy is there for you to access. Your emotions are touched with joy and optimism from your ruler, Jupiter. The Sun is still fighting with Mars, but this can now be used as energy which drives you forward to connect and learn from others who are grounded and practical.

Wednesday 3rd

Mars and Venus are at odds. You may find that you argue with members of the opposite sex. You don't have to explain your deepest thought processes to everyone, as they won't understand. Intense emotions cause you to probe deeply and look to the wider world for answers.

Thursday 4th

Today can be tricky as the Moon sits opposite the two disruptive planets, Mars and Uranus. You may find that the only way you can deal with things today is to switch off and enter a dream world which is yours alone. Retreat for now and regroup later.

Friday 5th

Be very careful out there. The Moon squares off with Mercury retrograde, and you may find that your mind and emotions cause you some difficulty. It's possible that you say the wrong thing to the wrong person or cross a line and make someone else uncomfortable. Be ready to apologise.

Saturday 6th

Venus meets Saturn. She will smooth over anything that seems impossible to overcome and encourage you to take baby steps in order to reach your personal summit. You don't have to do this all in one day. Watch how she acts as your cheerleader and reward yourself at the end of the day.

Sunday 7th

Today you may feel like you have taken a step backwards. Neptune, your inner compass, is evading you and communications are strained to make you overthink everything. Try to get some time with friends to round the weekend off in a relaxing way. Kick back and do something you enjoy.

Monday 8th

Mercury has nothing to say. He is busy receiving downloads for the next part of his onward journey. You must do the same and look, listen and take note of any messages that come your way today. They may be subtle dream symbols or blatant information from outside.

Tuesday 9th

You can get a glimpse of your true north as the Moon connects nicely to Neptune. Hold that close as you may feel undermined or ridiculed by someone in your social groups. There is no need to justify yourself to others but it's OK to defend your right to dream and expand.

Wednesday 10th

As the Moon drops into your hidden sector, you may have conflicting feelings throughout the day. You may withdraw then reach out, be selfish then selfless. Go with the flow but try to avoid upsetting others with your changeable moods as Mercury and Mars are at odds too.

Thursday 11th

There's a New Moon and this Moon meets Mercury retrograde. Emotions can be highly unstable, and accidents may occur if you are not alert. Venus meets Jupiter, which is very lucky, but you may miss out on a good opportunity if you concentrate on the negatives.

Friday 12th

The Moon enters your sign now. You may become self-centred after the instability of the last few days. It's possible that this may manifest in you allowing yourself a treat which is out of your price range, but you buying it anyway. This is a short-term gain which may cause strife in the long run.

Saturday 13th

Neptune is the theme of the day. Your co-ruler wants you to have some fun or switch off time. Self-indulgence may be a problem, as you may not know where to stop. Use energy from Neptune to look at your life through a different lens today.

Sunday 14th

If there are any mishaps thanks to Mercury retrograde, they are sure to be big. Jupiter says hello to Mercury, and Jupiter likes things huge. He may go easy on you as your ruler but be warned, Jupiter expands all he touches, including your waistline, so be conservative if you can.

Monday 15th

Today you're more prone to getting your planner out and filling it up. You need to be involved in action to feel good. Great connections to both Saturn and Jupiter in your hidden sector can help you see the value in structure, planning and lawfulness.

Tuesday 16th

While you're fired up to begin new projects, Venus is ensuring that you don't tire yourself too easily. You have a better idea of how to manage your time and energy today. This may not be so easily done, as someone from your social groups may place unreasonable demands on you.

Wednesday 17th

Saturn and Uranus are having a standoff, and today it reaches its peak. You may notice that communications are restricted or blocked. This may make you irritable and you could throw a tantrum. This is not a good look; try to calm down and take a breath.

Thursday 18th

The Sun enters your sign, so this is your birthday month. Expect your persona to have more charm than usual. You may attract more hopeless romantics into your circle now. When the Moon meets Mars, you may feel moody or sexy. Which way will you roll?

Friday 19th

The celestial lovers, Venus and Mars, aren't friends today. Expect to come across some tension between members of the opposite sex. This will certainly involve your conversations, and you may be stubborn and refuse to bury the hatchet. This may cause something to vanish from your life or be changed forever.

Saturday 20th

Today you may be extra chatty and inquisitive. Your family sector may be busy with a lot of gossip or exchanges of information. This is an easy-going weekend for you, so enjoy it with your nearest and dearest. You may even learn something new from a younger family member.

Sunday 21st

Mercury turns direct today. You may feel the release of tension, and can now think about contracts or commitments you have avoided recently. You are drawn towards the future and eagerly make plans for vacations or short trips. This is a great time to think about long term goals.

Monday 22nd

Do what feeds your soul today. For you, this is likely to be something artistic, musical or romantic. You may find that the gold hidden in your psyche comes up, and you find a way for turning this into a creative project. Surprise yourself and give it a go.

Tuesday 23rd

Today there's lovely energy for you to dream to your heart's content. You may be deeply emotional and project your feelings onto a love interest. Just be careful not to get carried away and smother a lover with your best intentions. Remember that there are personal boundaries for a reason.

Wednesday 24th

Your slushy mood may turn sexy. What's the harm in treating the one you love to a good meal, good music and your company? There's a danger of coming on too strong, so bear that in mind. Intuition can be strong, so listen to what it has to say.

Thursday 25th

Venus swims into your sign and becomes the ethereal mermaid. You may find that she's hard to catch and, likewise, you may be more idealistic and moodier than usual now. Other planetary aspects are not so easy and may cause some confusion. Make sure you keep one foot on the ground today.

Friday 26th

Your ego may be inflated today as you glide along with Venus. The Moon illuminates your stage and you put on a show. Nobody likes a show-off, so step down and be humble. There's a time to roar, and this is not it.

Saturday 27th

A Full Moon in your relationship sector throws light over your closest relationships. What has come to completion in the last six months? Something may surprise you under this lunar month, as Uranus gets in on the action. There is perhaps a wild card that you had not considered before.

Sunday 28th

A huge amount of earth energy keeps you grounded today. This may not feel so good to a water sign, and you look desperately to Neptune to take you away. Use this energy to simply get jobs done, catch up with people, and then do your own thing and drift away.

MARCH
· · · · · · · · · · · · · · · · ·

Monday 1st
The balance you achieve today may be more internal. The Moon connects nicely to the planets in your hidden sector, and you begin to make more sense of the shifts happening there. The road map becomes clear to you now. Accept the twists and turns you're about to experience.

Tuesday 2nd
Today you're optimistic and cheerful. Your inner and outer lives appear balanced and your deep yearning for something more is satisfied. You realise that the quest you've been seeking is presenting itself. The Holy Grail resides within you.

Wednesday 3rd
An intense Moon in your travel sector now helps you to understand that you must navigate your own territory before seeking the wider world. You may feel some rumblings from Uranus, who asks that you reach out and learn everything you can about the deeper mysteries of life, however uncomfortable.

Thursday 4th
Material from your psyche continues to surface and you may feel resistant or reluctant to explore this today. You might try to hold on to the more surreal aspects and ignore the hard work. Mars enters your family sector, and you may see cross words and disagreements at this time.

Friday 5th

Mercury and Jupiter meet again in your hidden sector. You may experience a head so full of chatter that you can't think straight. Alternatively, you may do your best thinking now, as Jupiter will have big ideas for you. Remember that he also blesses you, as your ruler, with joy. Welcome happiness in from wherever it comes.

Saturday 6th

There's lovely energy today that connects your thoughts to action. The Moon in your career sector helps you to combine your inner work and social status. Perhaps you have found a way of processing that reaches out to teachers and guides. Draw on old skills and interests now.

Sunday 7th

As the Moon dips into your social sector, try to enjoy some time with friends. Work colleagues may provide entertainment for you to participate in. Get talking and put some ideas out there. You may come up with some outside-the-box thinking that your social groups will benefit from.

Monday 8th

Hard work competes with dreaming today. Emotionally, you're committed to your responsibilities, but you still tend to wander off and enjoy your fantasy world. There's no harm in this if your duties are all done, but don't risk dreaming on the job if you have deadlines to meet.

Tuesday 9th

The Moon meets Pluto and you sense that familiar niggle which asks you to change, transform, or to otherwise let go of something. You're not very good at this, so start by making a small change today. This may be as simple as doing an exercise routine or walking rather than taking the lift.

Wednesday 10th

Today, the Sun meets Neptune. You may see any confusion or delusions burn away under the Sun's rays. Your true north, your inner compass and guide, will be most accessible to you now. Your co-ruler calls you to re-align yourself. You may have more confidence today.

Thursday 11th

The Moon in your hidden sector meets Mercury and your head and heart have a talk. You may need to have some quiet time to process thoughts before this evening, when the Moon enters your sign. A poor connection to Mars makes late thoughts aggressive and you may be too hard on yourself.

Friday 12th

Today it's possible that you've achieved a lot just by communicating with others. You may find that one good idea after another presents themselves and you're on a roll. These need to be grounded in reality or put on paper before you change your mind

Saturday 13th

A New Moon in your sign is a fantastic opportunity for you to set big goals and intentions. This Moon meets Neptune, and you may already feel absolutely certain of your path in life. Pluto intervenes to help you let go of that which is holding you back from success.

Sunday 14th

Venus also meets Neptune today. Self-love and compassion, combined with empathy for your fellow travellers in life, are high today. You're driven, responsible and geared up with your action plan. This is a great start to your new personal quest. Remember this feeling for when you are less positive.

Monday 15th

Your mood continues to be upbeat as you start the week with confidence. You may find that this rubs off onto others, and you share feelings about what you value in life. You may be an inspiration to those in the workplace today. Well done you.

Tuesday 16th

The Sun in your sign connects well to Pluto today. This will make any changes easier, as you will see the long-term benefit. Mercury comes into Pisces armed with all the knowledge you need to work on self-improvement. Your mind will be very busy with filtering information now. Make the most of it.

Wednesday 17th

You might see your stubborn side today. There's a possibility that you will come into conflict with someone, and this could very end unpleasantly. Think of a bull refusing to move but, when it does, you must quickly take cover. Be a slippery fish and get out of the way.

Thursday 18th

Planetary connections confirm that you must stick to your guns. This may be the beginning of the letting go process. Removing something from your life that no longer serves will free up some room for new growth. Make sure this is just and fair before you act.

Friday 19th

Conflict within the family is possible today. Once again, this may be necessary in order to shift perceptions or dismiss illusions that have existed for a long time. Saturn makes sure that you remember your responsibilities and only act if it's beneficial to the family group as a whole.

Saturday 20th

The Spring Equinox occurs today and acts as a springboard off which you may initiate new plans. Feel into the tension before making a move. Jupiter is supportive and you may find that plans become huge. Neptune, however, prefers a more flexible approach. Wait until you get a green light.

Sunday 21st

Venus leaves your sign and becomes the warrior goddess in your finance and value sector. She will help to bring in the funds but also to spend them. She will add her touch of balance, harmony and beauty to the plans you implement now. Have conversations and brainstorm ideas.

Monday 22nd

Today the energy is milder and may make you feel that something is missing. A sensitive Moon in your creative sector connects to Mercury and you may now look at recent ideas with a more intuitive mind. You may be defensive or even overprotective of your plans now.

Tuesday 23rd

Friends may try to be helpful, but you'll likely perceive this as interfering. The Moon opposes Pluto and you might feel some hurt or grief over what you have recently let go. Neptune adds a surreal touch to make you extra moody. You could benefit from time alone today.

Wednesday 24th

Today you should have found your voice and fired up again. An empathic sign like you can't deny a natural instinct to protect others, but you use it to stand loud and proud by yourself. You may ruffle a few feathers by your insistence on speaking your mind and not being dumbed down.

Thursday 25th

The Sun and Venus are together in your finance and values sector. Today would be best spent checking your bank balance and looking at how to improve your finances. You may have a double blessing today, so use it wisely. Thinking does not bring solutions today, action does.

Friday 26th

The Moon enters your relationship sector, just in time for the weekend. You feel like taking comfort with someone you know well who can help you sort through the finer details and make more sense of things. Two heads are better than one; there is no need to struggle alone.

Saturday 27th

Confusion and foggy thinking could cause you to halt and delay any work you do today. This is a quickly passing phase, but will influence how you proceed. Pause and reflect, listen to the words of a helpful person and wait until you have clarity. You may be forced to see another point of view.

Sunday 28th

A Full Moon lights up your intimacy sector and you get the big picture of what's been happening for you in the last six months. Have you been attempting to reconcile parts of your life that don't belong together? Deep issues attract and concern you, but may be wrong for you.

Monday 29th

Good connections to planets in your hidden sector help you to understand why balancing your inner life must come before putting it out there in the world. Difficult conversations may be had, but you should be able to manage this with skill and tact. Well done.

Tuesday 30th

Your inner journey continues to draw you with a promise of reward. Mercury meets Neptune and, if you listen to your inner voice, you may hear what that reward will be. You may need to concentrate and resist the urge to swim off to a fantasy island.

Wednesday 31st

Today you're more positive, as you have re-aligned yourself and will prove that you are worthy of a prize after hard work, but the work must be done first. This may weigh heavy on you. Is it a load that you are willing to carry? Do you accept this challenge?

APRIL
·················

Thursday 1st
Is there anything that you can transform today with regards
to your career? You may be facing deadlines and are well
equipped to tackle them under the planetary energy. Pluto
helps and you could hit the day running. Your sense of duty
and responsibility is strong, and this momentum might help
get all jobs done with ease.

Friday 2nd
Under this productive energy, you can communicate with
others and tweak long-standing problems to find a solution.
This is a day when you have blessings to draw on, and will feel
satisfied when you see things come to completion. You have
the right mind in order to tackle what comes your way.

Saturday 3rd
Take a day of rest today, you deserve it. Your mind and heart
aren't in sync and this is telling you that you need some down-
time. You may have burned yourself out with your recent
productivity. Later today, joining with friends can be fun.

Sunday 4th
Mercury leaves your sign and is fired up with lines of enquiry
he wishes to pursue. Your bank balance, home, and what
you find valuable, will all be under scrutiny now. You might
be stirring up interest within your wider groups and new,
innovative plans are forming. These may be slow to take off.

Monday 5th

The Moon meets Pluto, and you may find that you're emotionally charged to find the good in something which you have deemed a lost cause. This afternoon, your generous sense of duty to the wider world may see you putting in some effort to a global project.

Tuesday 6th

Today you may find that you're feeling rebellious. Something has surfaced from your unconscious and you need the whole world to know about it. Saturn pulls you back and reminds you of your duty to yourself before all else. Get all the facts before joining a revolution of sorts.

Wednesday 7th

Venus and Mars make a helpful connection and this energy brings your compassionate and warrior sides together. What has caught your attention? What are you incensed about? You may see a legal issue that you believe to be unfair. Be respectful if you choose to probe deeper.

Thursday 8th

Today you may find that you look back at times past, such as times when you may have used a skill or talent. Is it possible that you can use it again now? Your conversations may be unusual, but don't disregard them as there may be something useful you can take from them.

Friday 9th

The Moon in your sign meets Neptune. This is your chance to re-align or re-group with your goals and intentions. Mars connects badly and you may find that you're questioning the futility of some of your dreams. Part of you wants action, and part wants to dream bigger and bigger.

Saturday 10th

If you listen to elders, teachers or authority, you may find that you can benefit from their wisdom. This can be a project that may evolve into something bigger and include many of your friends and associates. Mercury turns your thoughts towards being a responsible citizen of the world.

Sunday 11th

Your emotional charges are activated now when the Moon meets Mercury. Your thoughts race and your heart tries to catch up. Something has really gripped you and given you a mission to do something in the wider world. Take in any information you can and sort through it later.

Monday 12th

A New Moon in your finance and values sector meets Venus, who likes money. This is an important sign that the goals and intentions you set now can be financial and have a good chance of manifesting. You may need to change your way of thinking about wealth and what that means to you.

Tuesday 13th

Communications may be volatile today, as your heart is speaking openly now. Not everyone will be on your side and you may find that hard to understand. What you are driven to achieve today is still only in thought-form. Don't let your ego get the better of you.

Wednesday 14th

You take a sideways glance at your true north and may doubt yourself today. Venus is about to leave your finance sector and urges that you don't leave anything unfinished. You may worry more today or be extra stubborn about doing things your own way. Slow down if you can.

Thursday 15th

The Moon shifts into your family sector which may make for a noisy few days. Venus enters your communications sector and will smooth over any difficult conversations you may have. She may even get you to do a short course of study which will ultimately benefit your growth.

Friday 16th

Today you may be reluctant to make any sort of change. Your social circle is the issue now, perhaps someone in your wider circle is pushing their weight around and you need to evaluate your connection. This may be difficult for a sensitive soul like you.

Saturday 17th

Tricky energy may tire you today if you try too hard to conform with others. There may be much to process, and you may not get any clarity. Mercury is busy connecting, but you may experience this like too much information coming your way. Leave it until tomorrow when the energy changes.

Sunday 18th

Mercury is thankfully silent now. He is in the heart of the Sun and receiving new downloads. You must do the same. Be still and listen or observe. Your intuition is on alert now, and you may surprise yourself with a few revelations. You are more sensitive to outside energies today.

Monday 19th

Mercury enters your communications sector. Watch how he can help you extract the information you need while he's here. The Sun joins him. You may see that these energies help you to expose liars and be perfectly clear when speaking and listening. This is because you slow down to absorb everything.

Tuesday 20th

Your energy moves from being inwards and intuitive to wanting to be bold and brave. Don't do anything rash today, as it's unlikely that it will go well. Connect with others and be of willing service to them. People will love your energy and want to be around you today.

Wednesday 21st

You must remember not to be pushy with others. Your communication style may not suit everyone, and you may tread on a few toes. Check in with your health today and give yourself a full examination. You tend to overlook your own needs when caring for others.

Thursday 22nd

Today is a good time for connecting with a partner or someone who is important to you. The Moon makes great connections to the Sun and Mercury, making this a perfect time to get to know someone deeper. Mars may make you overstep a personal boundary, so watch out for this.

Friday 23rd

If you've remained respectful with a partner, then today can be very exciting for you. Mars shifts into your sensitive, creative, romantic sector, while Venus and Uranus hook up. There may be champagne and fireworks on the agenda for you.

Saturday 24th

Come back down to earth today. You may have floated off to a fantasy land with a special someone. Be very careful this evening, as there's a possibility that you probe too deeply and cause tension. You may also reveal something shocking about yourself. Try not to cross any personal boundaries and you should be fine.

Sunday 25th

Mercury and Venus meet up, but both square off with Saturn. This means that your love talk may clash with your inner work, and you may have to balance it back up again. If you have compromised your self-respect, this may be difficult to rectify today.

Monday 26th

You may be able to redeem yourself today. The Moon is in your balancing intimate sector and aims for clarity. You may be sensitive or protective about a love interest. Jupiter also helps to trigger your generous and charitable nature. You may need to apologise, and this will do you good in the long run.

Tuesday 27th

A very intense Full Moon happens in your travel sector. This can be very difficult, as your travelling is mostly in your heart, mind and soul. Your personal journey may be attacked by others who perceive you as wasting time. You must find someone who truly understands you today.

Wednesday 28th

Pluto turns retrograde today. This will occur in your social sector. As Pluto asks for change and transformation, you may find that your duties, responsibilities and role in the collective will change over this time. Be a good Pisces and go with the flow.

Thursday 29th

You have a chance to prove yourself in the workplace today. No job seems too small or big. You enjoy a challenge and may well be presented with one which you take up and relish. Saturn is impressed at how you rise to this challenge, as it may well help with your inner work and self-improvement.

Friday 30th

Electrically charged energy is in the air today, when the Sun meets Uranus. This acts as a powerhouse in your communications sector. You may find that you're working from morning until night or chasing a deadline. By evening you'll be pleased with yourself and can enjoy some downtime with friends.

MAY

....

Saturday 1st

The Moon makes no contacts today, so you may enjoy a time where emotions are kept at bay. You may find this is unnatural but it will help you to concentrate and make decisions using logic and reason. The Sun and Uranus are still providing fuel in your communications sector.

Sunday 2nd

You may have managed to talk yourself out of an awkward situation, or persuade others to your point of view. By this evening you may feel exhausted and long for time alone. Indulge in something which will make you feel yourself again. Neptune suggests an aromatic salt bath.

Monday 3rd

The monthly meet up between the Moon and Saturn comes after a particularly trying weekend. You may wish to strengthen your own personal boundaries now. Self-care is paramount and will lift your spirits. Don't beat yourself up, praise yourself instead.

Tuesday 4th

Mercury flies into your family sector. He will be at home here and will bring much-needed laughter and merriment. You may feel some guilt around taking time for yourself. You can return to your empathic and connecting activities when you are fully recovered. Look after number one for now.

Wednesday 5th

Family issues may disrupt your solo time today. This may make you over-emotional, so be careful how you respond. It's likely that you see things as bigger than they are. Step back and remind people that you need time to yourself. You still have a lot of thinking to do.

Thursday 6th

The Moon is now in your sign and you're beginning to feel like yourself again. You get a glimpse of your inner sense of direction and feel satisfied that it's always there for you. Connection is important to a Pisces, so use Neptune as your anchor. Check your finances today.

Friday 7th

Your mood has lifted, and you're inspired to act on some of your goals and intentions. Emotionally, you stand between a desire to indulge and a need to transform. Is it possible to combine these two energies and give yourself a makeover today? A friend may offer an interesting suggestion.

Saturday 8th

You know what you want to do today but may have trouble getting started. Mars is at odds with the Moon and can be a drain on your resources. Your romantic, creative side is acting on intuition, and you may not trust this. Today you prefer to be more practical.

Sunday 9th

Venus makes her way into your family sector. She will attempt to harmonise any conflict here. It's possible that she will also get you brainstorming ideas for money-making schemes. You may clash with someone from your social groups today as you stubbornly refuse to conform to their will.

Monday 10th

You may be feeling lazy or slow today. There are many chores waiting for your attention, but you find that you procrastinate. As a result, you may be rushing around and catching up with them well into the night. Do what is essential and leave the rest for tomorrow.

Tuesday 11th

A New Moon in your communication sector explains why you felt stuck or slow. Something has ended or wound down and now you can begin again. Use this opportunity to make plans which will take time to develop as these are more likely to succeed. Don't be tempted by idealism.

Wednesday 12th

The Moon and Venus have a lady's chat in your family sector. This energy suggests that you pay special attention to females in the family today. They may share their wisdom with you. You have much more energy to get things done now. This could be a romantic day.

Thursday 13th

Your head and heart are in sync, and you may be eager to implement some new ideas of yours. These are influenced by your dream future and may not be fully formed yet. Jupiter moves into your sign and instils you with a huge urge to connect to everything and everyone.

Friday 14th

There may be so much going on in your head that you completely miss the collective wisdom from your family. Your individual life path is not in line with their goals, and this is OK. Just be sure to remain respectful to them, as they may only be trying to help.

Saturday 15th

Today you may be inspired to do great things. Your romantic, creative side is touched by the Moon and connects to Jupiter who, you should remember, makes everything bigger. You may have found the right words to create beautiful poetry. You're very sensitive towards the need of others at this time.

Sunday 16th

Today the energy suggests that you may feel warrior-like and protective over something. This could be something you have created, but don't feel ready to show to the world just yet. You may be impatient or irritable as you wish to share something you value. Hold on just a little longer.

Monday 17th

Pluto is causing a few hiccups in your social calendar today. There may be disagreements or passive-aggressive behaviour going on. Use the power of persuasion to get around a problem and restore harmony. You may be willing to put yourself out far more than others, and this will not go down too well.

Tuesday 18th

A battle of wills may occur today. This will come from within you and will concern your private life and your outward life. You may desire to impulsively speak out about something you find unjust, but your inner voice is telling you to sit down and be quiet.

Wednesday 19th

Listen to the words of the family today. Small children may say something which makes you think twice. Unfiltered communication could come as a surprise. The Moon opposes your ruler, Jupiter, in your sign, and you may find that your closest relationships are tense today. You want your own way now.

Thursday 20th

The Sun enters your family sector now. Expect a month of fun, laughter and revelations. Anything hidden will be exposed. You may find your romantic relationships difficult and prefer to have time away from them. Stick to family duties today, if you can. Avoid unnecessary conflict and lie low.

Friday 21st

Your dreams and aspirations seem far away, and this may cause you some upset and frustration. You may find that resistance is coming from your family area. It will be hard to communicate your deepest wishes to them. Your love-life may be more active and a source of comfort today.

Saturday 22nd

You may feel that you need to balance your ideals with those of another. It will help if you try to look at things from another perspective, and be as patient as you can. Keep emotions out of discussions today and aim for a clear line of communication.

Sunday 23rd

Saturn turns retrograde in your hidden sector. This will mean that you spend the next few months evaluating your role in the collective and how it is of value to your personal growth. You may be more inclined to turn inwards and do the hard work Saturn requires over the summer.

Monday 24th

You may become very serious today, and have dark and negative thoughts. Jupiter will make your mood bigger and Uranus makes you impatient. This is the necessary disturbances which will eventually lead to your growth and self-development. Ignore it at your own cost; it's there to help.

Tuesday 25th

Saturn is already giving you a hard time. You may now realise that you need to learn something which is out of your comfort zone. However, there's enough water energy around for you to use your imagination and swim your way to the shore if you feel lost.

Wednesday 26th

A Full Moon shows up in your career sector. Your big ideas may have come to completion in the area of work and your social status. If there's still work to be done, this will become clear now. You may have to put personal goals to one side and be part of a team.

Thursday 27th

Today will not be easy if you have ideas that are out of your reach.
You may be torn between family and work responsibilities. Be
single-minded and attempt one thing at a time, or you may be at
risk of burn-out.

Friday 28th

The weekend arrives and you desire to have some fun with
friends. You may have plans to drink, eat and be entertained by
your wider social circle. Be warned that a connection to Jupiter
means that you may overdo things and regret it in the morning.
Try a different approach and seek out your most sensible friends.

Saturday 29th

Mercury turns retrograde in your family sector. Before he
does so, he meets Venus who promises to smooth over any
arguments and misunderstandings which may occur. You may
feel restricted or blocked and your creative impulses have no
outlet at the moment.

Sunday 30th

Take things easy today. The Moon dips into your hidden sector,
suggesting that your time is best spent alone. Process your
negative thoughts and aim to turn them around. How can you
fulfil your own needs and please others? Fill your own cup first
and you will be ready to serve.

Monday 31st

The Moon meets newly retrograde Saturn. Listen very carefully
to your inner voice and try to connect to your true north.
Saturn will teach you that your goals are attainable if you
play by the rules and stay realistic. Make a vision board and
safeguard your dreams.

JUNE

Tuesday 1st

Emotions may be larger than usual as you worry through the
night and early hours. There may be guilty feelings of not
having done enough for others. Relax, this is the time to be
with your own thoughts and needs. Breathe easy and you'll feel
more like yourself later in the day.

Wednesday 2nd

Venus moves into your creative, romantic sector. This hails
a great time of being sensitive, protective and desirous of
harmony, especially in your love interests. You may feel a
touch of excitement today via messages or phone calls. Feel
how your heart skips a beat.

Thursday 3rd

You may find yourself lost at sea but don't worry, Neptune
comes to the rescue and you see a lifeline. Your thoughts
may be muddled or disturbing and your confidence is low.
Towards evening you should find the courage you need
to make the first move or reach out to someone who has
interested you. Good luck.

Friday 4th

Remember that Mercury is retrograde as he may give you some
trouble today. Your inner compass is acting up, but this may
also be a sign that something new has caught your attention
and you have drifted off course. Saturn gives you a nudge in
the right direction. Follow him.

Saturday 5th

An active, outgoing Moon makes you stop and assess your relationship with money. Mars and Pluto need you to look at what you share and what is yours alone. You may find that subscriptions are outdated and need reviewing. You may feel stuck between two difficult and opposing points.

Sunday 6th

Settle yourself down and put in some serious work today. Luck is on your side if you pay attention to your own desires and those of the collective. You may be a pivotal person amongst your peers. Defend your passions and seek justice in all that you do now.

Monday 7th

Things may feel slow and plodding as you struggle to get everything done. If you try to up the pace you may get in a muddle and have a mini tantrum. Double-check all communication and make sure people are in understanding. Travel may be disrupted today so plan ahead.

Tuesday 8th

As the Moon shifts, it makes better connections to Mars and Pluto, the two planets concerned with permanent change. Mars wants you to march out and declare love not war. This isn't a good idea, so hold back until the time is right. Being impulsive now can go terribly wrong.

Wednesday 9th

Your family sector may be busy as you're emotionally attached to dealing with matters there. Saturn is watching how you deal with taking the pressure off others by offering a helping hand. This will be returned to you, so do the right thing and be responsible.

Thursday 10th

A New Moon in your family sector seems to have come at
the right time. You may need to say enough is enough, wipe
the slate clean and start all over again. However, this Moon
soon joins Mercury and you may have trouble getting full
agreement from others. Don't push it.

Friday 11th

Mercury is quiet. You may find that you've come to a truce
or a stalemate in family matters. You may be more sensitive
to rejection this afternoon but will find your voice and get
defensive by evening. Ensure that everyone is pulling their
weight. Don't do more than your fair share.

Saturday 12th

When the Moon meets Venus, you may find that female
company is soothing and nurturing. Alternatively, you may
have more passion for a love interest that deepens with the
lunar touch. This is supported by a nice connection to Uranus
suggesting surprises or unexpected delights

Sunday 13th

You're pulled back to your personal goals but feel blocked.
Leave it alone today or you'll end up frustrated. Mars in your
health and duties sector is asking that you find a healthy way
to release stress and frustration. Starting an exercise regime
while he is here is a great idea as it's sure to become routine.

Monday 14th

Your voice and actions need to be in sync. Don't go spouting off without acting or you'll be exposed for a liar and a joke. Someone may cause you some grief and tension, but you must walk away or learn to bite your tongue. Avoid conflict at all costs.

Tuesday 15th

Today you had best lie low. Your sensitive soul is in danger of being knocked back. Planetary energy is unstable. Be careful who you speak to about your deepest thoughts and feelings. They may not be trustworthy, and this can make you feel vulnerable in certain company.

Wednesday 16th

You wish to have quality time with a partner or person you admire. You may be relying on them to analyse recent events for you. This person can get to the bottom of anything and see every minor detail. Knowing something has been thoroughly examined on your behalf gives you some peace.

Thursday 17th

Moments spent trying to connect with your inner compass are futile today. You may try, but without luck. Remember that Mercury is still retrograde, and things are unclear. Focus instead on what's going on with your love life. Surprises, revelations and harmonising activities are waiting for you to discover. Create love or art with a partner.

Friday 18th

The mysterious side of life may fascinate you at this time, but you have a need to reconcile it with your own lived experiences. This may take the shine off these themes. Allow yourself to be drawn into intimate situations that further your knowledge. Open your mind.

Saturday 19th

Trouble with your romantic and creative pursuits may come from Saturn and Mercury connecting to the Moon. You may have gone deeper or further than you're comfortable with and need to withdraw. Come back to a place you feel safe and start again another time.

Sunday 20th

Your social status may be on your mind. Concerns about how you're perceived by friends may trouble you. Speaking out isn't the best answer today as you aren't being objective. Your ruler asks you to find the bigger picture and not look for details which will worry you more.

Monday 21st

The Summer Solstice is here, and the Sun moves into your romantic and creative sector. This will be a time of warmth and sensitivity. Your best work will be done now. Jupiter turns retrograde in your hidden sector and asks you to look deeper within for inspiration. Love is easy this evening.

Tuesday 22nd

Mercury turns direct. You may now get clarity on family issues and agreements can be made. Give it time though. Not everyone will be willing to compromise at first. Be fair as Jupiter is testing your sense of justice. Be the compassionate Pisces everyone knows you are.

Wednesday 23rd

Today you may experience some passive-aggressive behaviour within your wider groups and your romantic interests. This may make you feel like running off and doing your own thing, but this is a test. You must remember personal boundaries and make sure that yours are strong enough to keep you safe.

Thursday 24th

A Full Moon in your social sector illuminates issues in your wider groups and social friendships. You may notice how these issues are not in line with your true north. Some friendships may need to be lovingly let go if they diminish you or prevent your personal growth.

Friday 25th

Your co-ruler, Neptune, also turns retrograde. It's possible that you completely lose sight of your inner compass for a few months, but this is fine. This is the time to review and reflect before moving on again. You may find that some things need a tweak or a total overhaul.

Saturday 26th

Look carefully at friendships and love interests. You may have blurred the boundaries here and will need to re-establish them. Control issues may surface and make you uncomfortable. Don't despair, this will be a very valuable lesson for you. Better boundaries mean better relationships.

Sunday 27th

Venus moves into your health and duties sector. You may find that you're more willing to be of service and do work which brings you no personal reward. This is highly commendable, show off your compassionate side with new boundaries in place. Further tests from Mars and Uranus try to knock you from a peaceful spot.

Monday 28th

Troubling thoughts may keep you awake. Right now, things seem worse than they are. You switch between wanting to help others and do some good in the world and doing your own thing and working on your personal growth.

Tuesday 29th

After a lot of deep thought about how you can serve the wider world, you now come back to your own goals and intentions. There is nice, watery energy for you to connect to your own needs and think about the future you desire for yourself.

Wednesday 30th

The Moon in your sign meets newly retrograde Neptune. This will feel strange and you may feel lost. Learn to go with the flow and see where it takes you. Look at things from a new perspective and have plenty of patience. This will be highly beneficial to you in the future. Take all the time you need to re-align with a new viewpoint.

JULY

....

Thursday 1st

Today you may find a way to enhance your financial situation. Grand ideas come to you but be warned, they might be unrealistic and fleeting. You have a passion in your heart that you wish to express but this may be hindered by authority figures. This could be a frustrating day.

Friday 2nd

You have more of an idea on how to proceed with schemes. Mercury helps you to think things through and Saturn reminds you of your responsibilities. Your dreams now seem a little more attainable. Go after what you want but keep it real. Today you have a chance of success.

Saturday 3rd

Spend the weekend grounding your plans and make positive steps. Reach out to others who can advise and keep you from wandering into fantasy. Look at the legalities before embarking on a project which will take a lot of time and effort. Cover all bases before starting on this.

Sunday 4th

Frustrations come and go today. This will pass so stick with it. You may find it hard to keep your thoughts inside and speak out with a passion that unnerves some people. Use restraint and tact before unleashing your plans to the outside world. Be enigmatic for now.

Monday 5th

You see a glimpse of your true north, but through a slightly different lens. You may be more concerned with making big changes which benefit you in a sensual or tactile way. Money and your home environment are now factors to consider. You are inspired and creative. This makes you happy.

Tuesday 6th

Today you may have intrusive thoughts which are triggers of self-doubt. You will not get clarity however much you try, so put it aside and distract yourself. It's possible that outsiders or family are giving you conflicting advice and you're getting confused. Do something different or self-soothe.

Wednesday 7th

Your mind will be more at peace as the Moon shifts and makes better contacts. Mars and Venus help you to keep track of what you desire and how you're going to get it. You must remember not to be selfish now. Do this for the right reasons.

Thursday 8th

Moon and Mercury meet, and your heart and head are in sync. You may be more realistic and able to think rationally. It's possible that your intuition kicks in and you follow a train of thought or a gut feeling. Sensitivity and awareness help you process logically.

Friday 9th

This is a great day for any creative or romantic pursuits. You're on top form and anything you birth has a touch of magic within it. Uranus has woken you to a completely new way of doing things. Thinking outside the box will be easy for you.

Saturday 10th

A New Moon in your creative sector is the green light you've been waiting for. All that ruminating you've been doing is now ready to present to the world. Pluto agitates you in a good way and transformation is possible. This is the start of something big for you.

Sunday 11th

Mercury flies into your creative sector and will help you process thoughts and ideas concerning your new project. He may also act as a lover and teach you how to woo a love interest. Don't go too fast with this, you must remember to merge and connect with the utmost respect for others.

Monday 12th

Mars and Venus, the celestial lovers, are getting close. The Moon visits both. This happens in your health and duties sector and suggests that common regard for someone who can support your everyday activities is approaching. You may both be spiritual warriors looking for a shared vision.

Tuesday 13th

Pay special attention to people you encounter today; Mars and Venus are now together and can signify an important connection for you. Mutual willingness to serve or heal will be the theme. Look at what happens at work, the gym or in situations where you are happy to be of service to others.

Wednesday 14th

This is a great time for romance. Mars and Venus are still close, and the Moon is in your relationship sector. You may find that you have stirrings deep inside you which tell you how you feel about a certain person or event. Listen to them.

Thursday 15th

The Moon opposes your inner compass, Neptune. However, the connection made by the Sun makes you act more from your ego. You may need to balance your inner and outer lives today as something isn't adding up. Choose heart over ego every time. Allow yourself to shine but for the right reasons.

Friday 16th

You strive for balance but have too much information in your head. Decision making is difficult for you. There appears to be no emotional anchor on which you can rely or help you to think. This must be done with logic, reason and intelligence.

Saturday 17th

This is another nice day for exploring what the Mars and Venus connection meant for you. The Moon is in your intimacy sector this morning and reaches out for meaningful connection with others on a one to one basis. This evening you need to be aware of passive-aggressive behaviour and subtle manipulation.

Sunday 18th

You desire to connect more deeply and on an entirely new level. This may mean that you're exploring the outside world and wishing to broaden your horizons. However, this must have esoteric or philosophical attraction for you. Conversation stirs up new emotions you're unfamiliar with. Explore them.

Monday 19th

Neptune gives you another glimpse of your true north and direction in life. You may feel that this is changing all the time but look closer, it's you who's changing. Pluto in your social sector may bring new friends and associates your way. You have something to learn from them.

Tuesday 20th

You may be networking far and wide. Your job may require that you connect with foreigners. Mercury and Uranus connect in a way that suggests that learning a new language is a big possibility for you. This will certainly make your world bigger. What have you got to lose?

Wednesday 21st

You have another chance to consolidate a new connection. Shared interests will be a topic of discussion. There may be an opportunity to travel or learn something mysterious now. Astrology, psychology and foreign cultures will attract you. You may even have a yearning to do something worthwhile for the collective.

Thursday 22nd

Venus enters your relationship sector. This bodes well for new relationships where you desire to connect in a meaningful way and be of willing service. Your health may improve too while she's here. The Sun also shifts, and you may notice a more cheerful approach to your duties.

Friday 23rd

Today has energy which will intrigue you. Your social sector hosts the Moon and you feel changes happening. You may see old friends and acquaintances falling away to make room for those more in line with your personal growth. Look at this as a necessary adjustment, not a loss.

Saturday 24th

There's a Full Moon in your hidden sector. This will shine a light into your darkest places but will please you. You may see where there has been a positive change which you first found uncomfortable. Listen to your inner voice and accept the praise it gives you.

Sunday 25th

You may lack energy today so take a day of rest. Retreat and be alone with your thoughts. Mercury and Pluto are opposing each other, and you may feel some guilt or sensitivity towards home and work issues. Allow yourself to relax and refresh yourself for the coming week.

Monday 26th

The Moon drops into your own sign and meets Jupiter. You may be more empathic towards others now. You'll need to filter out what may feel sticky or a burden. Relationships may be tense as you still need time to yourself. A love interest may be too clingy.

Tuesday 27th

Neptune calls you to think about your dreams and wishes but you feel more like fantasising. You could be more emotional or detached than usual. People may leave you alone as they have trouble getting through to you. You may not be feeling very sociable.

Wednesday 28th

Jupiter retrogrades back into your hidden sector. You must now look at where your feelings of injustice come from. There may be triggers concerning this while he's here. Mercury flies into your health and duties sector to make sure that your voice is heard and that you're getting a fair deal.

Thursday 29th

Mars joins Venus in your relationship sector. He will add vigour and sex appeal to new relationships but may also entice arguments. He opposes Jupiter and this may mean that your first trigger arrives today. Note what upsets you and find the root cause. It may not be what you think.

Friday 30th

You may be full of action and plans right now but unsure of how to implement them. Try slowing down. There's a chance of accidents or unnecessary arguments if you insist on steaming ahead. Conversations may be exciting enough to appease your need for speed.

Saturday 31st

Today has difficult energy for you to navigate so consider
entertaining yourself in a different way. It may seem like you're
hitting a brick wall every way you turn. Take the hint and stay
at home. Cooking, yoga or sensual pleasures will be the best
activities for this weekend. Enjoy something different.

AUGUST
· · · · · · · · · · · · · · · · ·

Sunday 1st

Listen carefully to subliminal messages from the dream world, nature or coincidences. This is an important time to be still and observe the world around you. You may learn a major lesson concerning self-discipline and you will surprise yourself.

Monday 2nd

Today isn't easy. You may come up against conflict with a person in authority. It's possible that you have to repeat a lesson you thought you had already mastered. You may not be in the mood to compromise so don't even attempt to.

Tuesday 3rd

You may be pulled towards a possible future and put your thoughts to your family. Overall there will be support there for you. It's your love relationships that may put up some resistance. However, there's a workaround if you discuss this openly and come with an innovative solution.

Wednesday 4th

Don't try talking yourself out of your dream goals and aspirations. You may be regretting taking something on, even a hope. This is a passing phase and you're being triggered by old habits and conditioning. Look to your ruler, Jupiter for fairness and he may show you a way forward.

Thursday 5th

Be gentle with yourself. You have a creative urge that needs an outlet, and this may be a joint project or simply some tender loving with a special person. Your drive is connected to a love relationship, but you're feeling protective and defensive.

Friday 6th

Today your ego may get a bashing but this will wake you up from a misconception. You may be inclined to take advice from a partner. Friends and acquaintances could be difficult to deal with. Pluto asks for permanent change or the transmutation of something old into a brand-new way of existing.

Saturday 7th

This morning the Moon shifts into your health and duties sector. You may be feeling vulnerable and will want to have some down-time. Check in with your health, you might be overdoing things and starting to get burnt out. Give yourself some love and let people know how you feel.

Sunday 8th

A New Moon in your health and duties sector is your chance to lay the law down and ensure that your own needs are met. This may upset some people but will ultimately benefit you. If you've had enough of being the go-to person, speak now.

Monday 9th

Mercury helps you to align your feelings with your emotions today. Good causes and underdogs attract you, but you must make a shift and learn to put yourself first. Jupiter opposes the Moon and you may struggle with not giving your all to everyone around you. You have limits too.

Tuesday 10th

The Moon meets Mars in your relationship sector. It's possible that you're extra touchy and argumentative. You may begin to feel stifled by a love relationship and believe that your dreams aren't there for you anymore. This is false, wait until the energy changes and your mood softens.

Wednesday 11th

As the Moon meets Venus you see the connection to a love interest improve. You may be feeling sorry for your recent rejection. There may be a conflict between meeting your own needs and those of your wider groups but remember that you can't pour from your own cup if it's empty.

Thursday 12th

Venus and Pluto connect to help you transform the old into something beautiful. You have a much more balanced outlook and understand where compromise can be mistaken for surrender. You may find common ground between yourself and a partner. Mercury enters this sector and opens up communication channels.

Friday 13th

The Moon is in your intimacy sector. You may find that your inner and outer worlds merge nicely. People are attracted to your empathic abilities, but you're beginning to realise the importance of personal boundaries. You don't have to be there for everyone, all the time.

Saturday 14th

This weekend may be intense. You may feel the need to expand your consciousness and look outwards for stimulation. It's likely that you rely on a partner to lead you in this as they will be able to see every detail and look for loopholes that you may not see.

Sunday 15th

Conversations may border on the taboo today. You may have bitten off more than you can chew in your quest to learn something out of your comfort zone. However, this is all part of your learning journey this year. You must experience discomfort in order to grow.

Monday 16th

Be mindful in the workplace. Tensions are high and you may experience cross words or misunderstandings. Venus moves into your intimacy sector to show you how beautiful it can be to share deep desires and fantasies with someone you trust. Be guided by her as she can also bring in some assistance with finances.

Tuesday 17th

You may be more optimistic now. Neptune is out of sight, but you have work to be getting on with and are more practically-minded. The workplace goals need attention and your mindset is on form to meet all deadlines. There may be praise at the end of the day.

Wednesday 18th

You may be more withdrawn than usual. Others will see it as a worry, but the truth is that you're driven to achieve things regarding your career. This may cause some concern to a loved one who may perceive that you're not interested. Reassure them.

Thursday 19th

Uranus turns retrograde. This may result in a few months of disturbances in your communications. Alternatively, this may also be a time of awakening for you. Mercury has met Mars in your relationship sector so be careful that your words aren't met with anger. Lively discussions may happen now.

Friday 20th

The Sun opposes your ruler, Jupiter. You may have another trigger regarding your duty to self versus your responsibilities in the collective. Saturn also reminds you to keep strong and healthy boundaries when dealing with disagreeable people. Control issues or manipulation may be a problem in your social sector.

Saturday 21st

There is crazy energy around, but it may be worthy of your attention. This influence can be fuel for revolution but also for genius thinking. You may find that innovative solutions are found for long-standing problems. Either way, this energy will certainly stir things up. Use it wisely.

Sunday 22nd

A Full Moon in your hidden sector will highlight the work you've done on yourself this year. You may have cause to celebrate or join with others to make a difference. Old habits may be replaced by better coping mechanisms now. The energy is volatile but exciting.

Monday 23rd

The Sun is now in your relationship sector. You may enjoy a more optimistic approach to connecting with others. Your personal relationships may benefit from a mutual desire to be of service and guidance. Your health might improve now too. The Moon in your sign keeps you mindful of your own needs.

Tuesday 24th

Today the Moon makes its monthly visit to Neptune. You might like to stand back and observe things from afar or at least with a different perspective. Discussions with a partner may help you to see things in a more methodical way. This will be much appreciated as it isn't your strong point.

Wednesday 25th

You're driven and motivated. You may prefer to keep things rational and logical right now as that approach is helping you get through the day. You have no time for anything deep and wish to communicate simple things with a partner without dreaming.

Thursday 26th

You may place value on objects or concepts that now need to be reviewed. Pluto asks that you take a good look at this and consider how much joy they are bringing you. It could be that your perception of value and worth needs to be changed now that you yourself have changed.

Friday 27th

Saturn teaches you another lesson. Slow and dependable is a better way to go about your business than rushing or being ethereal. Some of your ideas might need to be set aside as they have no real substance. Tackle jobs that are practical and enduring.

Saturday 28th

There may be some sort of shake-up or re-organisation going on now. Mars, Venus and Uranus are playing a game which involves your love life and your unpredictability. Expect the unexpected and go with the flow. Resistance is futile. You may experience the earth moving today.

Sunday 29th

Helpful connections to the Moon make any change easy. Discussions with a lover may prove to be the most effective way of bringing about necessary transformation. You might also find that a lover is on board with your bigger dreams and visions. This will be highly beneficial in the long run.

Monday 30th

Mercury moves into your intimacy sector indicating a time where you are willing to listen as well as be heard. You could also find that your conversations become deeper and erotic. Family issues need your attention, but this is of minor importance as all are agreeable and well.

Tuesday 31st

Put your dreams to one side. Your inner compass is unavailable to you, but this is fine; there are other things to see to. You may be driven to achieve something within your family sector and a partner may help you out. This may be legal business.

SEPTEMBER
· · · · · · · · · · · · · · · · ·

Wednesday 1st

You may be feeling creative or romantic but have trouble with clear thinking. A conflict occurs between free-thinking and a more structured approach. You require a balance or at least a heavy discussion which helps you to organise your thoughts. Go with your heart and see what you come up with.

Thursday 2nd

Surprise yourself and think outside the box. You might find an unusual resolution for a troublesome project. This may go against the grain and cause you inner tension with your desired path in life. Finding an outlet for that tension will produce exactly what you are after.

Friday 3rd

You've been looking at things through a different lens recently and it's now beginning to make sense. It's not as far away from your true north as you first thought. You may be more driven when you realise this. Let transformation happen. This is a blossoming of a talent you never knew you had.

Saturday 4th

You're prone to speaking your mind and going above and beyond your duties to please others. There will be a moment when you stop and check in with yourself. Is this conducive to your growth? Are you returning to old ways of behaving and relating to others?

Sunday 5th

Venus helps to remind you that your first duty is to yourself. As an empathic soul, you may find it uncomfortable to consider this. Your ruler is watching how you manage this. Try to find a way of helping others which doesn't leave you diminished.

Monday 6th

The Moon dips into your relationship sector where you can lean on a special person for support. Pluto shows you that relinquishing control, even for a moment can do you the world of good. This doesn't sit well with you and you may fret about it. You desire more balance in your intimate relationships.

Tuesday 7th

A New Moon in your relationship sector is a great chance to evaluate your one to one partnerships. Are they bringing you joy or adding stress to your life? You may feel irritable and provoke unnecessary arguments. Reaching out to Neptune for safety proves useless. You must use logic and reason.

Wednesday 8th

This morning you're more rested and sensible. Your dreamy, idealistic mind has calmed, and you may be sorting through issues where you may have pushed too far. Alternatively, you may have been pulled into something you weren't ready for and now need to retreat. Do what's best for you.

Thursday 9th

The Moon meets Mercury which usually means that your heart and head are in sync. Today, however, you may find that the noise inside your head is making everything more complicated. It's possible that you feel overwhelmed. Friends and lovers aren't helping right now, you're on your own.

Friday 10th

Venus spends her last day in your intimacy sector. She asks that you review her time and look at what you've learned. It's critical that you do this before she moves into your seductive travel sector and takes you to places you might not be ready for.

Saturday 11th

Emotions may spoil your day if you're not careful. The Moon is in an intense sign and opposes volatile Uranus. Your only lifeline now is Pluto who suggests that you do something practical and grounding. Bringing your work home may help. Stay away from fantasy thinking and mind-altering substances today.

Sunday 12th

Your relationships may stabilise you today. Your partner might know how to bring you back to land when you're swimming away from the shore. Allow yourself to be cared for by someone who's responsible and trustworthy. Don't waste the remainder of the weekend being stressed.

Monday 13th

The working week begins and the best thing you can do is to be productive. Mercury can help you to prioritise your chores and get a lot done. You have no time for dreaming today and this helps. Simply get on with the nitty-gritty of everyday life today and dream tomorrow.

Tuesday 14th

The Sun opposes Neptune and burns away any illusions you may have had. It's possible that you have a wakeup call and rise to action. This afternoon you need to get to the bottom of something deep or the top of something big. Good luck, you can do it.

Wednesday 15th

Mars enters your intimacy sector. This influence may improve your sex life or induce arguments so tread carefully. Conversations may border on the taboo today and shock you or others around you. Be careful who you speak to as not all will appreciate this topic of conversation.

Thursday 16th

Who is controlling who? The Moon in your social sector could be showing you where you have acquaintances with big influences over you. These may not be as helpful as you think. Neptune reminds you of your aspirations. They aren't forgotten, just being assessed and re-worked for the moment.

Friday 17th

You may have some worrying thoughts which keep you awake. Venus might be making you selfish and secretive now and she squares off with Saturn whose lesson she is disrupting. You will need to get back in line with the important task of building healthy boundaries. Egotistical behaviour doesn't suit you.

Saturday 18th

As the Moon is in your hidden sector it encounters Jupiter. This learning curve may appear to differ greatly from Saturn's teaching. Jupiter asks that you expand your mindset and reach out in different ways to merge and connect whilst Saturn asks that you observe personal relational boundaries.

Sunday 19th

Back in your own sign, the Moon makes helpful connections to Venus and Uranus. You're being asked to awaken and know your own desires. However, the planet of love only wants the best for you. Explore a spirituality that's more attuned to your personal goals and intentions. Educational courses may help.

Monday 20th

There's a beautiful Full Moon in your own sign. Take this moment to look within and congratulate yourself on the work you've done so far. The Moon joins with Neptune to let you have a good look at your future path. Pluto celebrates your transformation.

Tuesday 21st

Your body and mind may be extra tired today, but your heart knows what it wants and is happy. You're learning to put yourself first and this pleases Saturn. Look at what you value and use today to organise these into priority. You might find that some of these no longer serve you.

Wednesday 22nd

The Sun enters your intimacy sector and heralds the Autumn Equinox. This is a time of balance. Take time to pause and reflect on the past year before descending into the darker, more introspective nights. There could be a deeper lesson waiting for you.

Thursday 23rd

You may be action-orientated but find that there are roadblocks impeding your progress. Look at themes regarding yourself and relationships as these will surface now. Check your finances and those you share with another as they may be up for review too. There might be difficult conversations to be had today.

Friday 24th

The Moon meets volatile Uranus. Today can be tricky for you to navigate so go slowly. Accidents are more likely so stay alert and do one thing at a time. Alternatively, you may find something that rocks your world view and are inspired to act.

Saturday 25th

You might get a sideways glance at your inner compass and get pulled off task today. Mercury turns retrograde tomorrow so use today to make all the necessary preparations. Double-check travel plans, back-up all devices and make sure that your communications are understood.

Sunday 26th

Mercury will retrograde in your intimacy sector now. Pay special attention to deep and meaningful conversations as they are likely to be misinterpreted and make you uncomfortable. Family time can be fun today with extra activity to take your mind of other worries. An elder may have good advice for you.

Monday 27th

Your mind may be swimming with plans and ideas. The environment around you could be too noisy for you to concentrate so don't even try. It's likely that you're drifting off to a fantasy world in order to escape current situations. Simply enjoy some uncomplicated time if you can as this will lift your spirits and make you laugh.

Tuesday 28th

You may feel the first effects of Mercury retrograde today. This occurs in your family sector but will not be too problematic. It might just be that you hear some gossip or instructions that get muddled along the way. You may also attempt to shock others with wild stories.

Wednesday 29th

Venus connects to your inner compass and seduces you away. This can result in some excellent art, music or writing. Your intuition is strong now so use it productively. Uranus connects to suggest that you have something new to put down on paper which may even surprise you.

Thursday 30th

There's so much water energy that you'll feel at home and in your comfort zone. You may find a muse and your creative urges will be on top form. This influence is also great for any new romantic pursuits. Mercury retrograde may have a few tricks up his sleeve today.

OCTOBER

. . . .

Friday 1st

Mercury retrograde challenges Pluto today. You may see some unsavoury activity within your friendship groups. It's likely to be secretive, nasty and maybe malicious, causing a rift within the group. Your inclination is to join in and make your point. You could be the peacemaker now if you choose.

Saturday 2nd

Tensions are still high but there's a slim chance you may be able to withdraw from it all. Venus helps to make any losses or permanent changes in your social circle a little easier. You might find that they're not such a big loss after all.

Sunday 3rd

As the Moon enters your relationship sector, you may desire to spend time with a partner who exudes common sense and virtuousness. They could help you to see the bigger picture and details you might have missed. Time alone to process your thoughts will also be of value to you later today.

Monday 4th

Expect the unexpected. This may come in the form of a surprise from your partner in an attempt to cheer you up. You've lost sight of your inner compass, but this is fine. There's no point dwelling on possibilities when there's more urgent work to be done.

Tuesday 5th

Pluto and Venus once again make good contacts to the Moon. This means that you can make changes or deal with judgements with a little more compassion. This afternoon your sense of fairness makes a decision easier to make. Emotions can be put aside, and you use logic and reason.

Wednesday 6th

A New Moon meets Mars and Mercury retrograde in your intimacy sector. This can be quite intense as Pluto turns direct too. Something has permanently ended and here's the new start you've been waiting for. Just don't sign any commitments yet. Actions begun after the retrograde are more likely to stick.

Thursday 7th

Venus enters your career sector. She'll show you the joy of bringing harmony and optimism to the workplace. You may turn inwards now and do some introspection. Plant seeds of ideas to enhance your knowledge of deep and philosophical thought. Spiritual matters attract you now.

Friday 8th

The Sun meets Mars today. This is a powerhouse of energy for you to access and use in your intimate sector. You might see this as confirmation of the goals you set at New Moon. An intense Moon stirs something up inside you and you may wish to share this with someone close.

119

Saturday 9th

Mercury meets Mars and the Sun. Be very careful as your mental faculties may be foggy or too rash. There's also the chance of accidents or burn-out now. Spend time with women in the workplace as female intuition is strong today and they can produce miracles.

Sunday 10th

Saturn turns direct. This is good news if you've been paying attention to his lessons. He will relax his grip on you and your hidden sector will experience a heavy weight being lifted from it. A green light tells you to make haste and get on with a new project.

Monday 11th

You may sense some hesitation within your wider friendship groups. The truth has come out and you could see false friends drop away. Teachers and leaders may expose themselves as fake. Maybe it's just you awakening to a new level of awareness. Think about it.

Tuesday 12th

There may be a further shift or a bright idea forming in your mind. It's possible that you're thinking in another way and wish to share this with a friend or group. Don't be shy, people welcome your ideas and will appreciate that you've participated in the group.

Wednesday 13th

Today's a lucky day as you see something of your true north, but this time you're seeing it with a responsible, disciplined mind. You may have disregarded pie in the sky ideas and have now come around to basing your plans on thoroughly grounded, practical concepts.

Thursday 14th

The Moon meets newly direct Saturn in your hidden sector. Consider this as a call to the headmaster's office. You'll get a full report of your activities this year. He will tell you if you've passed the test. Other planetary aspects are favourable. You may be pleased with yourself.

Friday 15th

Both Sun and Moon connect to your ruler. Jupiter's luck-bringing qualities are available to you but not in a direct way. Open your mind and take on board any subtle messages you receive. Jupiter strokes your ego and hits an emotional trigger to which you need to react.

Saturday 16th

Today you may take an overdue rest and allow yourself some downtime. The Moon in your sign makes you pause and reflect on the past and future. You may feel challenged, but you may also take this opportunity to bring old skills back into use for your future goals and aspirations.

Sunday 17th

Your ruler turns direct. Mark what happens which can enhance your growth and let you reach out to the wider world. The Moon sits with Neptune so you might get a good idea of how this will pan out for you. This energy is too good to ignore. Use it or lose it.

Monday 18th

Mercury also turns direct. You may feel light as a feather and choose to enjoy some free time doing nothing much. Look around you and evaluate your possessions and what they mean to you. You might declutter and feel even freer. This would be a worthwhile activity.

Tuesday 19th

The Moon is challenged by newly direct Mercury. You are asked to look at what may need to be rectified to give you peace of mind. Money matters need attention. Look at subscriptions which may no longer be active. Investments you share with another might be accessed.

Wednesday 20th

A Full Moon in your finance and values sector confirms that you need to look at your bank balance. It's possible that you've overspent or missed important payments. However, the opposite is also true, and you may have increased your balance.

Thursday 21st

Watch your temper today. Saturn and Uranus are making it difficult for you to hold your tongue and you don't want to undo all the good work you've done this year. Play by the rules and if someone is provoking you, bid them farewell. Enjoy a little luxury today if you can.

Friday 22nd

Mars and Pluto are squaring off and you may see more arguments within your social sector. This may change the way you put energy into groups as you realise that they're not in line with your best interests. You may have an emotional reaction to something you thought you had dealt with.

Saturday 23rd

The Sun enters your travel sector. Prepare to be enlightened about subjects you've previously thought nothing of. This may be a time where you change your ideas about other cultures and wish to discover more about religion, philosophy or deeper subjects such as astrology and psychology. Enjoy some family fun this weekend.

Sunday 24th

Talk to your nearest and dearest about your role in the family and at work. You may receive some good advice from siblings. Help is available if you need to balance your home and work duties. You may enjoy both areas more if you slim down your responsibilities.

Monday 25th

It may be futile to get back on your personal path today as other issues demand your attention. There's much joy to be had from working on your personal issues as Jupiter is now in the position to help you move along quickly. You receive courage and energy from Mars to enter unknown territory.

Tuesday 26th

Work duties might exhaust you and take you far away from your goals. This may make you extra sensitive. You desire to be creative or pursue your love interests but there's no time left in the day and this may upset you.

Wednesday 27th

Your heart and mind may feel separated. Your default is to go with your heart, and you could find that you're drifting off into fantasy land or ignoring your practical responsibilities. This is a frustrating time for you. You will need to be adaptable and go with the flow.

Thursday 28th

Stand up for yourself. Don't let yourself be dragged into other people's dramas. You may be called upon to mediate a situation, but this isn't your job and it may drain your energy. Send love to those suffering but opt out of being the one to fix them.

Friday 29th

You have the gift of the gab and can persuade people to do anything. Be mindful of your conversations as there's a possibility that you engage in a discussion which others aren't ready to hear. You may shock someone with your outspokenness.

Saturday 30th

Today you may yearn for time with a partner. You want some time where you are cared for or even seduced. Mars moving into your travel sector opens up avenues for exploring the dark and mysterious sides of life. You need a travel guide and your partner is offering their services.

Sunday 31st

Allow yourself some quality time with someone you love and admire. They may have a way of solving problems which hasn't occurred to you. You might find that you have mutual regard for each other's views today and you can be a force of strength when together.

NOVEMBER
....

Monday 1st
The pace is picking up now. There could be issues regarding money that need your attention. This may involve a partner or group of people. You have a good sense of responsibility and your major chores get done easily. Don't worry if you have no time to dream. Today is for practical matters.

Tuesday 2nd
Mercury and Pluto are at odds today. You may have difficult conversations with someone or bring something to a permanent end. Saturn graces you with the tact needed to approach this and come to the best possible outcome for all. This will free up some mental space.

Wednesday 3rd
You may be having second thoughts or regrets. The Moon and Mercury meet up and you could experience turmoil. Overthinking is possible and this will have an emotional attachment. Just be fair, there's not much more you can do. Don't stress about things you can't control.

Thursday 4th
There's a New Moon in your travel sector. This may set you on a path of deep discovery via long-distance vacations or higher education courses. This Moon makes some touchy connections and will possibly stir up something you now need to deal with once and for all.

Friday 5th

The Sun opposes Uranus and affects your style of conversation. You may hear or speak some shocking words. Venus and Mercury both change signs and you might feel the shift as a desire to connect with people outside your normal circle. Your mind is extra inquisitive now. What do you desire to know?

Saturday 6th

The energy today suggests that you're swimming into unknown waters and looking around. New friends could come along just in time for the festive season. Keep your eyes and ears open for anything that's seductive or exotic. You may decide on dining out this evening to satisfy that craving.

Sunday 7th

The Moon connects to both of your rulers. Neptune is evasive and not showing your personal quest which means that Jupiter is getting all your attention in your hidden sector. You might not even notice what important inner work you achieve today but it will be big.

Monday 8th

The Moon meets Venus and the energy is feminine and intuitive. This may affect your wider friendship groups or your social status at work. Other aspects suggest that you're willing to go the extra mile and make something happen today. It's possible that you're planning a social event.

Tuesday 9th

Be very careful as you may feel manipulated or controlled.
Alternatively, it's you who is fully in control. The emotional
Moon meets Pluto so this could go two ways. Neptune seduces
you and you might take a step or two to re-aligning yourself
with your personal quest.

Wednesday 10th

The planetary energy is volatile so watch your step. You
may experience arguments, personal attacks or a complete
change of mind by someone close or in authority. You will
probably not escape any of this, so do your best to stay
calm, kind and respectful.

Thursday 11th

Any tension today will be magnified by the Moon meeting
Jupiter. There may be many triggers which will test you
beyond your comfort zone. You will need to assess whether
the best option is to submit or stand up for yourself. Do what's
right for you and gives you the least stress.

Friday 12th

The Moon dips into your sign and you may feel more like your
usual self. This is a good time to pause and do nothing as you
might not be sure how to move next. Take some time out and
connect with your wider groups. Online associates could give
you the distraction you require.

Saturday 13th

Breathe deeply and let it out. You've found your inner compass again and feel back on track. Mars and Mercury offer you the energy and mind to learn something which will benefit you. However, Uranus sits opposite so mind how you proceed as it may have unexpected results.

Sunday 14th

Use today to check that your finances are healthy. You may wish to invest or claim back money from a long-standing fund. Overspending is also possible now, but you feel justified and deserve it. Big plans for the season are being made and you may be the coordinator.

Monday 15th

Someone may not be playing nicely in your social sector. A rift between friends is likely. Disharmony amongst your friends or work colleagues makes things awkward today. This doesn't sit right with you. Do the responsible thing and your conscience will be clear.

Tuesday 16th

There are important changes going on. This could also be passive-aggressive or secretive behaviour. It may provoke your sense of justice and you wish to sort it out. You might try to step in and mediate. Step back, as there's a chance it isn't your business.

Wednesday 17th

Mars opposes Uranus and this almost definitely means that you experience conflict. Conversations by mouth, email or messaging may get nasty. This could also involve money, relationships or joint investments such as taxes, inheritance or other shared responsibilities. Don't sleep on it, sort it out before it becomes too stressful for all parties.

Thursday 18th

The tension continues. Mercury tries to help by giving you the power to speak and offer other perspectives. However, you're dealing with personalities that are stubborn and resistant to any peace offerings. This will be a tough day, hang in there and try to stay afloat.

Friday 19th

The Full Moon in your communications sector brings recent matters to a head. You may find an obvious solution now or decide to draw a line and let things go. You simply want the peace restored and may compromise your principles to achieve this. Rely on family this evening.

Saturday 20th

You just can't please everyone all the time. It's commendable that you try hard to do this, but you may have to accept defeat. Later you may look back and realise that this was the best possible move to make. Others will need to own their roles in this upset and move on.

Sunday 21st

Spending time with your family will bring you pleasure today. Light-hearted chatter may be a relief after the recent tension you have had. Neptune is hiding from you and you perceive this as a challenge. If you can discuss future plans with family then do so, but if they don't understand, don't take it personally.

Monday 22nd

The Sun moves into your career sector. This will have the effect of making you investigate enhancing your work prospects and possibly travelling. There may be a way of combining both. This is a good day for romance as Venus and Mars are connecting well.

Tuesday 23rd

Be creative today. There's a wash of watery energy available for you to wallow in. Romance, art, music and spiritual matters are all highlighted for you. You may have to choose between being a nurturer or a lover, but this is all part of your adaptable nature.

Wednesday 24th

Mercury enters your career sector. Maybe this is the time to ask for a raise or a different, more research-based role. You're sensitive and protective of what you value. It's possible that a new romance or art project isn't ready to be announced to the world.

Thursday 25th

Today you may do your own thing in your own way and ignore consequences. You're feeling braver now and have something you would like to show off to the world. Venus and Mars are connecting well so this is likely to be something that you're very passionate about.

Friday 26th

What you want for yourself and what you want for the wider world is at odds today. You're torn between making a selfish move and one that benefits the wider group. You do so much for others, you deserve this moment. Don't feel guilty about it.

Saturday 27th

The Moon moves into your relationship sector, but you may be hesitant to make any moves with a special person. You're afraid of saying the wrong thing or going too fast. It may be a better idea to quietly withdraw until you're sure this is what you want.

Sunday 28th

Your nerves are tingling, and you're alert to the possibility of something strange and new coming your way. This excites you but pulls you off course. The Moon opposes Neptune and you may be led astray by fantasies or false promises. Get a reality check today; ensure you know what you're doing.

Monday 29th

Mercury is in the heart of the Sun and is silent. At this time, you must turn on your intuition and listen for subtle messages. You're positive and uplifted so this shouldn't be too bad. The energy is looking good which comes as a relief after uncertainty.

Tuesday 30th

You aim for harmony today. Many of the planets combine to help you reconcile your inner and outer worlds. Deep feelings are surfacing now, and you may experience the return of old habits. Venus and Neptune make this a dreamy romantic day so make the most of it.

DECEMBER

. . . .

Wednesday 1st

Neptune turns direct. This is great news for you as you're now free to forge ahead and go after what you deserve. Prepare to swim in deep waters and connect with your true north. As your co-ruler, Neptune will let you explore and guide you to do your best work now.

Thursday 2nd

An intense Moon helps you to take the first brave steps you need to walk your own path. Choose your guides and helpers wisely. Don't be reckless. Uranus is disturbing the ground you stand on and you may experience shifts in your psyche that confirm you're on your way.

Friday 3rd

The Moon meets hot-headed Mars. Your passions are foremost in your heart. Jupiter is opening and expanding your mind but go slowly as this may be overwhelming. There is still the day to day work to do so don't neglect it. Your journey will accommodate all parts of your life.

Saturday 4th

There is a New Moon in your career sector. This will act as a starting point work wise. Perhaps there's a way that you can switch up your career goals and incorporate them into your new journey. This Moon meets Mercury so take the time to research and explore possibilities.

Sunday 5th

Today you're determined and responsible. You enjoy some time with friends but have the good sense not to overdo things. Enthusiasm and optimism make all that you to today a joy. Friends may notice this and try to knock you off your happy place, but you're too strong.

Monday 6th

Mars and Pluto connect to tear down old structures that are holding you back now. This may feel uncomfortable at first, but you might soon realise the benefits. Things will continue to shift as you adjust. Stay adaptable and this will be easy for you.

Tuesday 7th

The Moon meets Pluto and you feel an emotional pull to what has been released. Grieve this loss for the value it once held for you. Give gratitude for the space it has now made. This afternoon your altruistic side makes you reach out to a good cause as if to celebrate.

Wednesday 8th

You may come across authority figures or leaders who attempt to pull you back into line. That is their line, not yours. You might need to be firm and politely decline their misguided but well-meaning advice. Remember that personal boundaries need to be healthy and strong.

Thursday 9th

Talking to new friends or acquaintances may help to confirm your new choices. You may have a moment of doubt and feel a little stuck. This is just a passing phase so relax and if need be, take some time alone with your thoughts if friends confuse you even more.

Friday 10th

The Moon is in your sign now and gives you some peace. You can use this time to get back in touch with your body or spirituality. Yoga, meditation or walking in nature may help. Little things will excite you as you feel your way on your journey.

Saturday 11th

Venus and Pluto meet up. This can herald a tricky situation where you may feel manipulated or controlled. You might not know how to react. As the Moon meets Neptune you're advised to be patient and maybe look at things from a different perspective. Don't be tempted to act just yet.

Sunday 12th

You may be itching to do something which you feel validates your choices and path. However, the planetary energy suggests that you need more time to evaluate the world around you as you're looking at it through different eyes now. The time for action will come soon.

Monday 13th

Mars moves into your career sector and Mercury into your social sector. As the festive season fast approaches this may simply mean that social engagements and work deadlines are coming in. Alternatively, this can also mean that you network far and wide. Researching a new interest is always a good idea before acting.

Tuesday 14th

Today you're practical and methodical in all that you do. You can feel that things are going too slow but at the end of the day, you will see that you did your work well. You may have to decline a social engagement and do overtime to meet deadlines.

Wednesday 15th

You may be a bit sensitive today as you have no time to dream or study your personal interests. The Moon meets Uranus and your mood could be close to erupting into tears. This could also be burnout, so slow down, breathe and believe in yourself.

Thursday 16th

You're being advised to look after number one today. You may be feeling the pressure of trying to forge your own path and being coerced by others to join in some fun. This might not be to your taste right now and you prefer to lie low with family. Polite refusals are needed.

Friday 17th

The Moon sits opposite Mars. This may mean that you see issues or conflicts arise between people of the opposite sex. You could also have difficulty balancing both your work and family duties now. Something has to give; choose what is best for you alone.

Saturday 18th

You feel cast adrift as you try to re-align yourself. Don't worry, Neptune hasn't abandoned you, there are simply other more pressing things to think about today. Enjoy a time of family chores and visits which will make the festive time special. They're counting on you to be part of it.

Sunday 19th

A Full Moon occurs in your family sector and shows you the full scope of your achievements with your kin this year. Venus also turns retrograde. You may see the return of an old lover, a breakup or troubling relationships with women now.

Monday 20th

Your creative and romantic urges come out. You'll need to factor in some time to be with a lover or get musical, poetic or artistic. This will come easily and you will find your muse. This Moon opposes Mercury so things may be unclear at first, then there will be no stopping you.

Tuesday 21st

The Winter Solstice arrives and gives you an opportunity to pause and reflect before the mayhem happens. Give gratitude for the lessons you've learned this year. You may find that you are humble and more accepting of differences within the family at this time.

Wednesday 22nd

Today you're on top form. There's a lot of preparation to do and duties to perform. You love to serve others and today you do this with extra cheer. However, an elder in the family or your wider interest groups may have something to say to derail you.

Thursday 23rd

Your ruler Jupiter returns to the very last part of your chart. He's at the end of your hidden sector and asks that you check in with your deepest self today. Is there something that you've forgotten about or put to one side? Maybe the seasonal duties have caused you to neglect something important.

Friday 24th

Tension and arguments are possible today. The Moon is in your relationship sector but connects to planets which can be volatile. Be careful out there as you may witness accidents and mishaps. Slow down and double-check everything. Get your partner to help with the details.

Saturday 25th

Venus retrograde has returned to Pluto's arms. You may experience this as unfinished business with a current or past lover. This could come as a passing comment that acts as a trigger. Uranus and Mercury help to make this a day full of surprises and laughter so don't dwell on the negative.

Sunday 26th

Time spent with a lover may give you both food for thought. You might have fond memories return to you. Sharing your dreams and visions with someone who is practical and dependable may help you to begin grounding them in reality.

Monday 27th

You should be able to enjoy a quiet day as the Moon is in your intimacy sector and aims for harmony. It's possible that something from your hidden sector comes up to be healed but this doesn't bother you and is perhaps a welcome insight into past behaviours. You're outgoing and personable today.

Tuesday 28th

Today you may experience something that rocks your happy boat. Be careful who you share things with as there could be secrets and jealousy around you. The darker side of life rears its head this evening. You might need to take cover. This will need investigating but maybe not today.

Wednesday 29th

Jupiter, your ruler, enters your sign. This is great news as he will stay for a year and enhance everything he touches. You will receive many blessings from the jolly planet who can enhance your joy, optimism and sense of adventure now. You will reach out far and wide over the next year.

Thursday 30th

Mercury meets Pluto. He's receiving his new mission to take forward into 2022. All will be revealed soon. You may have a secret rendezvous today, as Venus retrograde is currently connecting to a seductive Moon. Be safe and remember your personal boundaries.

Friday 31st

As the Moon meets Mars in your career sector, you get a boost of confidence about your work. You may be more driven to succeed in the new year. Your motivation can be high, and you're eager to get back into a routine. But first, enjoy any celebrations you participate in tonight.

Pisces

....

PEOPLE WHO SHARE
YOUR SIGN

PEOPLE WHO
SHARE YOUR SIGN

. . . .

No pinch can take the faraway sign of Pisces out of their dreamland. With their artistic flair, compassionate hearts, and wonderful imaginations, Pisceans can both inspire and heal. Whether it's sharing their visionary talents like Alexander McQueen and Jenny Packham, or emotional lyrics like Kurt Cobain and Johnny Cash, the gifts from Pisceans can help restore a magic to the world. Discover which of these enchanting Pisceans share your exact birthday and see if you can spot the similarities.

20th February

Rihanna (1988), Miles Teller (1987), Trevor Noah (1984), Chelsea Peretti (1978), Kurt Cobain (1967), Cindy Crawford (1966), Walter Becker (1950), Ivana Trump (1949), Mitch McConnell (1942)

21st February

Sophie Turner (1996), Riyad Mahrez (1991), Ashley Greene (1987), Ellen Page (1987), Mélanie Laurent (1983), Jennifer Love Hewitt (1979), Jordan Peele (1979), Michael McIntyre (1976), Kelsey Grammar (1955), Alan Rickman (1946), Nina Simone (1933), Hubert de Givenchy (1927)

22nd February

Drew Barrymore (1975), James Blunt (1974), Chris Moyles (1974), Jeri Ryan (1968), Steve Irwin (1962), Kyle MacLachlan (1959), Julie Walters (1950), Niki Lauda (1949), Robert Kardashian (1944), Bruce Forsyth (1928)

23rd February

Dakota Fanning (1994), Skylar Grey (1986), Andre Ward (1984), Aziz Ansari (1983), Emily Blunt (1983), Josh Gad (1981), Kelly Macdonald (1976), Daymond John (1969), Kristin Davis (1965), W. E. B. Du Bois (1868)

24th February

Earl Sweatshirt (1994), O'Shea Jackson Jr. (1991), Priscilla Chan (1985), Floyd Mayweather (1977), Bonnie Somerville (1974), Billy Zane (1966), Steve Jobs (1955), Phil Knight (1938)

25th February

Eugenie Bouchard (1994), Rashida Jones (1976), Chelsea Handler (1975), Sean Astin (1971), Téa Leoni (1966), George Harrison (1943), Anthony Burgess (1917), Pierre-Auguste Renoir (1841)

26th February

CL (1991), Charley Webb (1988), Teresa Palmer (1986), Erykah Badu (1971), Max Martin (1971), Michael Bolton (1953), Johnny Cash (1932), William Cody (1846), Victor Hugo (1802), Christopher Marlowe (1564)

27th February

Lindsey Morgan (1990), JWoww (1986), Kate Mara (1983), Josh Groban (1981), Chelsea Clinton (1980), Peter Andre (1973), Li Bingbing (1973), Derren Brown (1971), Timothy Spall (1957), Elizabeth Taylor (1932), John Steinbeck (1902)

28th February

Sarah Bolger (1991), Olivia Palermo (1986), Karolína Kurková (1984), Natalia Vodianova (1982), Ali Larter (1976), Amanda Abbington (1974), Ainsley Harriott (1957), Paul Krugman (1953), Bernadette Peters (1948), Frank Gehry (1929)

29th February

Jessie T. Usher (1992), Mark Foster (1984), Ja Rule (1976), Pedro Sánchez, Spanish Prime Minister (1972), Tony Robbins (1960), Dennis Farina (1944)

1st March

Justin Bieber (1994), Kesha (1987), Lupita Nyong'o (1983), Jensen Ackles (1978), Javier Bardem (1969), Paul Hollywood (1966), Zack Snyder (1966), Ron Howard (1954), Harry Belafonte (1927), Harry Winston (1896), Frédéric Chopin (1810)

2nd March

Becky G (1997), Nathalie Emmanuel (1989), Bryce Dallas Howard (1981), Rebel Wilson (1980), Chris Martin (1977), Alexander Armstrong (1970), Daniel Craig (1968), Jon Bon Jovi (1962), Karen Carpenter (1950), Lou Reed (1942), Dr. Seuss (1904)

3rd March

Camila Cabello (1997), Jessica Biel (1982), Ronan Keating (1977), Alison King (1973), Julie Bowen (1970), Ira Glass (1959), Miranda Richardson (1958), Zico (1953), Alexander Graham Bell (1847)

4th March

Brooklyn Beckham (1999), Bobbi Kristina Brown (1993), Draymond Green (1990), Whitney Port (1985), Chaz Bono (1969), Patsy Kensit (1968), Sam Taylor-Johnson (1967), Tim Vine (1967), Khaled Hosseini (1965), Patricia Heaton (1958), Catherine O'Hara (1954), Shakin' Stevens (1948)

5th March

Madison Beer (1999), Taylor Hill (1996), Sterling Knight (1989), Dan Carter (1982), Hanna Alström (1981), Jolene Blalock (1975), Eva Mendes (1974), John Frusciante (1970), Lisa Robin Kelly (1970), Joel Osteen (1963), Talia Balsam (1959), Esther Hicks (1948)

6th March

Tyler, The Creator (1991), Agnieszka Radwańska (1989), Shaquille O'Neal (1972), Connie Britton (1967), Rob Reiner (1947), David Gilmour (1946), Valentina Tereshkova (1937), Gabriel García Márquez (1927), Michelangelo (1475)

7th March

Laura Prepon (1980), Jenna Fischer (1974), Matthew Vaughn (1971), Rachel Weisz (1970), Wanda Sykes (1964), E. L. James (1963), Bryan Cranston (1956), Piet Mondrian (1872)

8th March

Stephanie Davis (1993), Petra Kvitová (1990), Kat Von D (1982), James Van Der Beek (1977), Freddie Prinze Jr. (1976), Florentino Pérez, (1947), Randy Meisner (1946)

9th March

YG (1990), Bow Wow (1987), Brittany Snow (1986), Matthew Gray Gubler (1980), Oscar Isaac (1979), Juliette Binoche (1964), Bobby Fischer (1943), Yuri Gagarin (1934)

10th March

Emily Osment (1992), Ivan Rakitic (1988), Olivia Wilde (1984), Carrie Underwood (1983), Samuel Eto'o (1981), Robin Thicke (1977), Timbaland (1972), Jon Hamm (1971), Sharon Stone (1958), Chuck Norris (1940)

11th March

Thora Birch (1982), LeToya Luckett (1981), Benji Madden (1979), Joel Madden (1979), Didier Drogba (1978), Johnny Knoxville (1971), Terrence Howard (1969), John Barrowman (1967), Jenny Packham (1965), Alex Kingston (1963), Rupert Murdoch (1931)

12th March

Christina Grimmie (1994), Stromae (1985), Jaimie Alexander (1984), Pete Doherty (1979), Aaron Eckhart (1968), James Taylor (1948), Liza Minnelli (1946), Jack Kerouac (1922)

13th March

Jordyn Jones (2000), Mikaela Shiffrin (1995), Kaya Scodelario (1992), Tristan Thompson (1991), Common (1972), Jorge Sampaoli (1960), Dana Delany (1956), William H. Macy (1950)

14th March

Simone Biles (1997), Ansel Elgort (1994), Stephen Curry (1988), Jamie Bell (1986), Taylor Hanson (1983), Chris Klein (1979), Brian Quinn (1976), Megan Follows (1968), Billy Crystal (1948), Michael Caine (1933), Quincy Jones (1933), Albert Einstein (1879)

15th March

Paul Pogba (1993), Lil Dicky (1988), Jai Courtney (1986), Kellan Lutz (1985), Eva Longoria (1975), will.i.am (1975), Bret Michaels (1963), Fabio Lanzoni (1959), Mike Love (1941), Ruth Bader Ginsburg (1933), Gerda Wegener (1886)

16th March

Wolfgang Van Halen (1991), Theo Walcott (1989), Jhené Aiko (1988), Alexandra Daddario (1986), Danny Brown (1981), Brooke Burns (1978), Sophie Hunter (1978), Alan Tudyk (1971), Lauren Graham (1967), Flavor Flav (1959), Victor Garber (1949), Jerry Lewis (1926)

17th March

John Boyega (1992), Hozier (1990), Grimes (1988), Rob Kardashian (1987), Edin Džeko (1986), Coco Austin (1979), Brittany Daniel (1976), Alexander McQueen (1969), Billy Corgan (1967), Rob Lowe (1964), Gary Sinise (1955), Kurt Russell (1951), Pattie Boyd (1944), Nat King Cole (1919)

18th March

Lily Collins (1989), Danneel Ackles (1979), Adam Levine (1979), Alex Jones (1977), Emma Willis (1976), Queen Latifah (1970), Peter Jones (1966), Vanessa Williams (1963), Grover Cleveland, U.S. President (1837)

19th March

Héctor Bellerín (1995), Garrett Clayton (1991), AJ Lee (1987),
Bianca Balti (1984), Eduardo Saverin (1982), Kolo Touré
(1981), Bruce Willis (1955), Glenn Close (1947), Ursula
Andress (1936), David Livingstone (1813)

20th March

Marcos Rojo (1990), Ruby Rose (1986), iJustine (1984),
Fernando Torres (1984), Freema Agyeman (1979), Chester
Bennington (1976), Michael Rapaport (1970), Kathy Ireland
(1963), David Thewlis (1963), Holly Hunter (1958), Spike Lee
(1957), Douglas Tompkins (1943), Fred Rogers (1928),
B. F. Skinner (1904)